The Alaska Geographic Society

THE ALASKA GEOGRAPHIC SOCIETY is a nonprofit organization exploring new frontiers of knowledge across the lands of the polar rim, learning how other men and other countries live in their Norths, putting the geography book back in the classroom, exploring new methods of teaching and learning—sharing in the excitement of discovery in man's wonderful new world north of 51°16'.

MEMBERS OF THE SOCIETY RECEIVE *Alaska Geographic®*, a quality magazine in color which devotes each quarterly issue to monographic in-depth coverage of a northern geographic region or resource-oriented subject.

MEMBERSHIP DUES in The Alaska Geographic Society are $20 for initiation and the first year, $16 thereafter. (Eighty percent of the first year's dues is for a one-year subscription to *Alaska Geographic.®*) Order from The Alaska Geographic Society, Box 4-EEE, Anchorage, Alaska 99509; (907) 243-1484.

MATERIAL SOUGHT: The editors of *Alaska Geographic®* seek a wide variety of informative material on the lands north of 51°16' on geographic subjects—anything to do with resources and their uses (with heavy emphasis on quality color photography)—from Alaska, Northern Canada, Siberia, Japan—all geographic areas that have a relationship to Alaska in a physical or economic sense. We do not want material done in excessive scientific terminology. A query to the editors is suggested. Modest payments are made for all material upon publication.

CHANGE OF ADDRESS: The post office does not automatically forward *Alaska Geographic®* when you move. To insure continuous service, notify us six weeks before moving. Send us your new address and zip code (and moving date), your old address and zip code, and if possible send a mailing label from a copy of *Alaska Geographic®*. Send this information to *Alaska Geographic®* Mailing Offices, 130 Second Avenue South, Edmonds, Washington 98020.

Second-class postage paid at Edmonds, Washington 98020. Printed in U.S.A.

To teach many more to better know and use our natural resources

ALASKA GEOGRAPHIC®

VOL. 5, NO. 1, 1977

COOK INLET COUNTRY

Editors: Robert A. Henning, Marty Loken, Barbara Olds, Lael Morgan, Jim Rearden, Betty Johannsen, Tim Jones, By Fish, Hank Rosenthal
Designed by Roselyn Pape

Overleaf — Mount McKinley, North America's highest peak at 20,320 feet, looms at the right, 135 miles north of Anchorage across Knik Arm. To the left is Mount Foraker, 17,400 feet. This view is from the foothills of the Chugach Mountains behind Anchorage, and shows only a northern portion of the city — biggest in the state with about 200,000 residents. (Pete Martin)

The tides of Alaskan history, and the tides that have made Cook Inlet famous for their great ranges between highs and lows, the frequent curling tidal bores, the back and forth crushing flow of winter ice have something in common. This is where the action is.

Eskimo and Indian and Aleut cultures met here in unrecorded history. Russian traders competing one with the other, settled in this region, mined the first gold, probably caught the first commercial fish. Explorers of several nations made early reconnaissances. Here is where the first modern Alaskan farms, so symbolic in American history as indicators of permanent western settlement, were cut from the wilderness. Here is where Alaska's first planned city was laid out. Here is where rail meets the sea, where roads end, where air trails to the world join.

On the streets, on the back trails, from sea to mountain fields of ice, there is action, romance of yesterday, challenge of tomorrow. People are doing here, against a backdrop of many things peculiarly Alaskan — doing and daring. Building.

From the headwaters of the Susitna to the sea bird-cluttered cliffs of Chisik Island, from the gateway through the mountains behind Palmer to the passes west of Cook Inlet, this is the Cook Inlet basin, where something like two-thirds of Alaska's population lives. An important region. Exciting.

This is where the action is.

—Robert A. Henning

Overview

"It's a country within a state," a long-time Anchorage resident said of the Cook Inlet basin. Whether or not the description was original with him, it was apt. Cook Inlet country is well defined geographically, economically and by climate — a distinctive region in a state so large you must always specify which Alaska you are talking about.

The region is neatly fenced all around by mountain ranges. Even the seaway entrance has a gatepost peak, Augustine Volcano, mounted on its own island. The Aleutian Range stands to the west of Cook Inlet, overlapping the Alaska Range, which then curves around to the north side. Midway in its long arc across the state, reaching toward the Wrangell and Saint Elias Mountains, the Alaska Range is intercepted from the south by the Talkeetnas. They form the northeast boundary before merging into the Chugach Mountains down the east side. The Chugach range goes its way along the Gulf of Alaska, but the Kenai Mountains corner into it and, as the southern boundary, stretch across the Kenai Peninsula to the mouth of Cook Inlet again.

The basin inside this frame is bigger than Indiana, or more than half the size of Washington state. It is home to almost two-thirds the population of Alaska, with 60% of that number joining in the urban sprawl that astounds first-time visitors to Anchorage.

The Cook Inlet basin is fenced in by dramatic mountain ranges, as this ERTS satellite photo reveals. Cook Inlet cuts through the center of the photo, ending in Knik Arm (top) and Turnagain Arm (reaching the edge of the photo to the right). The Aleutian Range parallels the west coast of Cook Inlet at lower left, blending at upper left with the Alaska Range, which arcs north and east to surround the Gulf Coast region. Kenai Peninsula and the sharp-edged Kenai Mountains are at lower right in the photograph, penetrated by 30-mile-long Kachemak Bay. (ERTS Photo)

Far left — **Chickaloon Flats is a shallow and muddy area near the north tip of the Kenai Peninsula, south of Anchorage across Turnagain Arm. The flats are an important migration stop for ducks and geese — as many as 20,000 Canada geese and 500 swans congregate there, and the area is used extensively by sandhill cranes during migration. (Nancy Simmerman)**

Cook Inletters — if such a term can be used to denote their specific status — live somewhat more comfortably than do some other Alaskans. It is not just because they are at the state's center of goods and services; nature also favors them. The encircling mountains shield against Pacific gales and the excessive rain, snow and clouds of northern coastal strips. At the same time, the 200-mile-long inlet brings the ocean's influence into the basin, modifying temperatures. The climate is transitional, between maritime and interior, or continental.

Dignified by their almost year-round snowcaps, the mountains all look tall. (Actually, the average height is only 5,000 to 8,000 feet, which makes the visible giants such as Iliamna, Redoubt, Foraker and McKinley — the tallest in North America at 20,320 feet — appear all the more impressive.)

Nevertheless, an example of how more-than-mile-high mountains affect the basin's climate is shown in the difference between Whittier, on the Gulf Coast, and Portage, only 13 miles away but behind the barrier to the southerly rain-producing winds. Whittier's average

Left — **The head of Turnagain Arm, viewed from Turnagain Pass, 59 miles southeast of Anchorage on the Seward Highway. Turnagain Pass (elevation 988 feet) is a popular recreation area for Cook Inletters — hiking in summer, skiing, snowshoeing and snowmobiling in winter. (John and Margaret Ibbotson)**
Below — **Canadian dwarf dogwood, or bunchberry (*Cornus canadensis*), is found in many areas of the Cook Inlet region, particularly in birch and spruce forests, and alpine areas up to subalpine zones. (Nancy Simmerman)**
Right — **Birch, not always as golden as this one, are found throughout the Cook Inlet region. Included are paper birch, Kenai birch, dwarf arctic birch and resin birch. (Nancy Simmerman)**

Left — **An impressive rainbow near Seldovia, photographed early one July morning. Seldovia is on an arm of Kachemak Bay, 16 miles southwest of Homer. (Neil and Betty Johannsen)**
Above — **Fireweed (***Epilobium angustifolium***) is abundant in the Cook Inlet region. (Nancy Simmerman)**

precipitation is 175 inches a year, enough of it in frozen form to account for 22 feet of snow. Portage's annual average is 58 inches, with 12½ feet in snow. Anchorage, in the middle of the basin, behind the coastal mountains, has about the same precipitation as Los Angeles, 15 inches, even though part of it falls as 5½ feet of snow during the winter.

The Cook Inlet region as a country was inhabited in early times along the same boundary lines. Long before European contact, Eskimos lived in the Kachemak Bay area and along the maritime strip as far east as Prince William Sound; later, the Athabascan-speaking Tanaina Indians took over the entire basin and its salmon streams.

Cook Inlet may look like one big channel that ends by splitting into 40-mile-long Knik Arm and 48-mile-long Turnagain Arm. In physical characteristics, though, it is almost two different bodies of water. The division between Lower Inlet and Upper Inlet is at The Forelands, where opposing fingers of land point at each other, one from the west shore (West Foreland) and one from the Kenai Peninsula (East Foreland).

On a map, the bottleneck appears to be a mild one. The inlet already is funneling, its volume forced from an average entrance high tide of 14 feet to 30 feet at Anchorage and even more in Turnagain Arm. The Forelands exert an additional squeeze, confusing tidal action in both parts of the inlet. In the Lower Inlet the current runs up the Kenai coast and circles down the west coast. Currents in the Upper Inlet also flow counter-clockwise, but in a separate "whirlpool" from the Lower Inlet. (See following page.) Between The Forelands the current averages 3.8 knots at the peaks of ebb and flow, but can get up to 6.5 knots.

Since all but a couple of the major rivers flow into the Upper Inlet, their waters join the whirling motion and dilute the sea. It freezes because of a high fresh-water content. Saltier Cook Inlet, below The Forelands, stays fluid. Much of the glacial sediment brought down by the rivers also circulates in the upper bowl, keeping it muddy and, in fact, threatening the eventual extinction of Knik and Turnagain arms as the particles settle out. Only the center of the Upper Inlet is as deep as 30 fathoms.

Anchorage is saved as a year-round port only by annual dredging, plus a nuisance that emerges as a scouring benefit — the extreme tides.

Left — **Bruin Bay, across Cook Inlet from the south tip of the Kenai Peninsula, 20 miles west of Augustine Island, is the site of some unusual geologic formations . . . and also the home of quite a few brown bears. Mike McBride, a Kachemak Bay lodge owner, offers some perspective on the size of this coal-laden anticline. (Mike McBride)**
Below — **Fishing for salmon from the shoreline of Homer Spit, Kachemak Bay. (Dan Kowalski)**

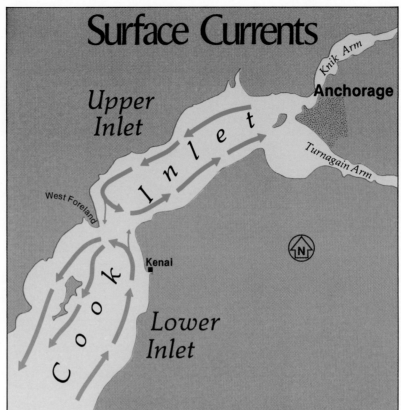

Surface Currents

In their drastic, twice-daily rising and falling (up to 30 feet), they break up the ice, allowing stout ships to trudge through the frozen shards.

What with such tides, turgid water and four months of ice, the Upper Inlet is not a place for marinas or salt-water sports fishermen. Salmon, shrimp, crabs, herring and clams do most of their thriving in the better-flushed Lower Inlet.

The geology of the basin and the surrounding ranges is described by geologists as complex. Small wonder. The whole coastal arc of Alaska, through the Aleutian Islands to the Southeastern Panhandle, is part of the Pacific Rim "Ring of Fire," characterized by tectonic activity. The grinding together of the earth's floating plates is accompanied by volcanism, uplifts, subsidence and earthquakes, all of which tend to change the landscape radically and sometimes suddenly.

Left — **Cook Inlet has been the state's leading petroleum producer (until start-up of the trans-Alaska oil pipeline in 1977), but the region's production may taper off in 25 years unless additional areas are exploited.** (Nancy Simmerman)
Below — **The 31-foot sloop *Nellie Juan* beats into a stiff headwind and choppy** sea on Kachemak Bay, one of Cook Inlet's most popular boating areas. (Neil and Betty Johannsen)
Lower right — **A party of butter-clam diggers at Kachemak Bay, on the Kenai Peninsula. Cook Inlet, south from the midpoint, offers many great spots for clamming — especially for razor clams.** (Nancy Simmerman)

An ancient sea covered Southcentral Alaska some 250 million years ago, but the general outline of the mountains began to appear soon after it receded. They came through uplift and volcanic intrusions, and went away by erosion two or three times. Seas penetrated valleys and later retreated. During the past million years, at least five glaciation periods have helped design the Cook Inlet basin, with ice sometimes almost a mile deep. For eons glaciers scoured the mountains and washed mud and sand into the bowl, and they still do.

The result was sand and gravel in layers up to 20,000 feet deep. Between ice ages and other adverse conditions, rather lush vegetation grew on the outwash plains. Buried in the cycles, it produced billions of tons of coal, at depths ranging from 3,000 feet to surface exposure.

Nonmarine sedimentary rock from the Tertiary period (1 to 70 million years ago) also holds petroleum in layers up to three miles deep. It is possible that still older marine sediments can be tapped for oil and gas.

All the present oil and gas wells are either in Cook Inlet proper or are on the Kenai Peninusla near The Forelands, where most residents of the basin are glad to see them adding to Alaska's economy. Now, as leases extend still farther down the Lower Inlet, fishermen and ecologists have become unhappy. (In resource-rich Kachemak Bay, the state has changed its mind about oil and gas developments, buying back oil-lease sites to prevent possible harm to the area.) Discontent is advanced by Alaska's loss of its suit in the dispute over whether Lower Cook Inlet is under state or federal supervision. The decision was that "the channel is too wide. It's not inland waters, and therefore does not belong to the state."

Still, Cook Inlet has a stake in further discoveries, because according to guesses by those in the industry, present oil production and its petro-chemical spin-offs may start petering out in 25 years.

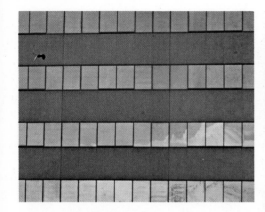

Left — **Anchorage drivers head home at dusk. (George Herben)**
Above — **Reflections of the Chugach Mountains in the windows of a newer Anchorage office building. Anchorage is one of the only towns in Alaska that was not founded because of mining, fishing, fur trade or other natural resources. (Lael Morgan, Staff)**
Right — **Railroad construction, beginning in 1914, launched Anchorage; it's been a transportation and supply center for Southcentral Alaska ever since. (Third Eye Photography)**

Petroleum developments do not have to happen just in Cook Inlet, of course, to be of importance to Anchorage. It is Alaska headquarters for the oil companies involved in North Slope production, the building of pipelines and petroleum exploration elsewhere in the state. There is little transitory appearance to the office buildings and hotels that continue to rise, or in the new shopping centers that sprout up to serve expanding residential areas, although some areas around town bear the marks of instant growth — acres of mobile homes.

It is the only city in Alaska that was not founded because of mining, fishing, fur trade or some other natural resource. Youngest of the state's cities, Anchorage lacks a glamorous past. It was urban from the start, in the sense that it began as a transportation and supply center, and it still is.

Railroad construction-camp tents were pitched in 1914 and the first permanent buildings went up the following year. Supplies could be landed from the sea in summer, and steamships refueled with coal from the Matanuska mines. The government-owned Alaska Railroad was completed to Fairbanks in 1923, but meanwhile it was hauling freight from the year-around port of Seward into Anchorage, where it also established headquarters.

Juneau held an uneasy lead as the state's biggest city until the Second World War, when Anchorage sprinted ahead, and its growth since then has made the race no further contest. All roads seem to lead to

15

Anchorage, whether aerial, marine, rail or paved. The port handled some three million tons of cargo in 1975, during a period of heavy activity on the trans-Alaska pipeline, and the railroad pushed two million. Airplanes carried 125,000 tons of freight to or from the international airport, while at least 20 interstate trucking firms hauled stuff into the city.

Alaska's small towns and villages do not have storage room for everything they need. They have to take shipments in quantities they can stow away, and Anchorage is their warehouse. As the principal distribution center in the North, the city handles more than three-quarters of the state's wholesale trade, and two-thirds of the retail business.

Statistics are for Greater Anchorage, but that term became more meaningful in 1975 when the City of Anchorage merged with the Greater Anchorage Area Borough to form the Municipality of Anchorage, which is now the governing unit for the entire 600-square-mile area.

From the top floor of a downtown high rise, the city *appears* to have plenty of room to grow, but the land supply in the bowl isn't all that good. Two huge military bases, Elmendorf Air Force Base and the Army's Fort Richardson, block expansion to the north and east. Where they leave off, Chugach State Park begins, and it and the Chugach National Forest extend well beyond the southern reach of Turnagain Arm.

The lower slopes of the Chugach Mountains might appear to provide nice view lots, but a large portion of the landscape that rises more than 500 feet above sea level is bedrock. The city's shelf is an alluvial plain in a patchwork pattern — sand, gravel, rocks, blue clay. Extensive bogs

Left — New buildings go up at a frantic pace in Anchorage, antiquating skyline photographs of the city every few weeks. Club 25, one of the oldest buildings in town, is now surrounded by the Hotel Captain Cook and the new Captain Cook tower. (Neil and Betty Johannsen)
Above — Times have changed since the summer of 1915 when Anchorage was little more than a tent town. The city's population is now at about 200,000, and some say it could reach 300,000 by 1980. (Phyllis Mithassel)

18

formed in depressions that once held lakes, and peat deposits run from 5 to 30 feet deep. More than a surface survey is needed for any land being looked at as real estate.

Most of the damage in the 1964 earthquake was in areas underlaid with Bootlegger Cove blue clay and materials that could compact from the shaking. The resulting earth movement was what amounted to a horizontal landslide, with slippage along the saturated clay toward the nearest unconfined edge. In Anchorage's case, that was the bluffs along the shore, where the clay surfaces.

The downtown quake-damaged area has been stabilized, a process that includes a subsurface drainage system. Use of similar areas is now subject to stabilization first, while strips of land along some bluffs are simply off-limits to building. (Lately, some buildings have gone up in areas that had earlier been believed unusable.) The rest of the Anchorage area is considered nominal risk, which puts it in the same classification as almost any other place on the quake-prone Pacific Rim.

Still, there's that ever-expanding population — 200,000 or so, and more expected in the very near future. There is a bit of inhabitable land at Girdwood, 37 miles southeast of Anchorage, and a fair piece at Chugiak-Eagle River, 14 miles northeast. A few miles farther is the boundary of Matanuska-Susitna Borough, with its big rivers entering the marshes of upper Knik Arm, its sometimes flat, sometimes rolling farmlands, and Wasilla Lake, Lake Lucille and Big Lake, plus smaller ones that entice summer residents.

Left — **Knik Glacier and gorge, in the Chugach Mountains northeast of Anchorage. In the background are Inner Lake George and Mount Muir, elevation 7,605 feet. (Nancy Simmerman)**
Above — **Another kind of gorge, running down the Seward Highway just after the 1964 Good Friday earthquake. The quake killed 115 people and caused massive damage to towns and villages in Southcentral Alaska. (Art Kennedy, Bureau of Land Management)**

Left — **The cemetery at Ninilchik, a small agricultural and fishing village on the Kenai Peninsula, 38 miles southwest of Kenai. (Neil and Betty Johannsen)**
Above — **House painting at Indian, 23 miles south of Anchorage on the Seward Highway. (Tim Thompson)**
Right — **The land squeeze in Anchorage has pushed developers farther into the hills and surrounding valleys. The city is running out of places to grow — surrounded as it is by mountains, parks, military bases and water. (Marty Loken, Staff)**

Here was Alaska's most promising agricultural land, and it is still the biggest producer of milk and most other farm products. However, the great Matanuska Valley colonization experiment of the mid-Depression 1930's did not work out quite as planned. For one thing, not enough farmers could make a living from their allotted 40 acres. The same thing happened over the years in Matanuska Valley as in the rest of the United States — fewer and fewer families operating bigger and bigger farms.

Large farms require hired help, but even city businessmen have trouble holding employees against the competition of other wages. Fertilizer, feed and machinery cost more than in the Lower 48. A constant stream of refrigerated and containerized cargo now flows on a steady schedule into Anchorage and its environs to be sold at competing prices.

So, Anchorage's land squeeze — and, importantly, the planned construction of a new state capital city near Willow — is producing a new crop in Matanuska-Susitna Borough — subdivision signs. Farmers own acreage in big enough chunks to interest developers. When one farmer sells out for more than the normal price of agricultural land, the valuation and taxes go up on what remains, further increasing pressure on others to quit farming and cash in.

The land squeeze in the region's pastures and population centers is now being felt in other areas — down the Kenai Peninsula, and in all other directions from the hub of Anchorage.

With most things on the increase — recreational needs, industrial growth, tourism — the face of Alaska's "country within a state" is rapidly changing . . . some say deteriorating, others say progressing.

Moving in for a closer look, we'll examine the region's five geographic provinces: The South Side, North Kenai Peninsula, Greater-Greater Anchorage, the Matanuska-Susitna valleys and The West Side . . . each an important and strikingly different region within the region. □

The South Side

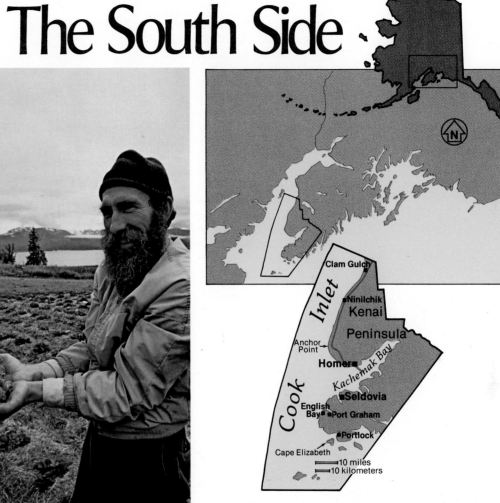

First stop in our counterclockwise tour of the Cook Inlet basin is the lower tip of Kenai Peninsula, a resource-rich country extending from the Barren Islands, on the south, to Clam Gulch on the north. In between is the recreation center of Kenai Peninsula, beautiful Kachemak Bay.

Left — A deserted cabin at Portlock, on the south shore of Port Chatham, 16 miles south of Seldovia; once a cannery site named for Captain Nathaniel Portlock, a British explorer who, along with Captain George Dixon, visited Cook Inlet in July 1786. Other early explorers in the area included Captain James Cook, Captain George Vancouver and — notably — a chubby Dane named Vitus Bering who, along with A. I. Chirikov, mounted the Kamchatka Expedition for Tsarist Russia and "discovered" Alaska in 1741. After visiting several islands in the Gulf of Alaska the two captains sailed north toward Cook Inlet; Bering's first landfall in the region was probably Afognak Island in the Kodiak group. Chirikov, on August 1, sighted Cape Elizabeth, the southeasterly gate to Cook Inlet, noting "high, snow-covered mountains on the land."
(Neil and Betty Johannsen)

Right — Homesteader Bob James of Homer, with fresh strawberries from his garden, which overlooks Kachemak Bay.
(Jim Rearden, Staff)

Right — Port Graham, illustrated during Captain Nathaniel Portlock's 1789 voyage to the Cook Inlet area. (Alaska Historical Library)
Lower right — English Bay, at the south entrance to Port Graham, 10 miles southwest of Seldovia, was originally the Russian post of Alexandrovsk. Population of the village was 78 in 1970. (Gil Mull)
Far right — Ruins of an old salmon-processing plant at Portlock, an abandoned community near the southern tip of the Kenai Peninsula. The cannery was moved to Port Graham in the late 1950's. (Neil and Betty Johannsen)

Below — Log rafts at Jakolof Bay, at the south end of Kasitsna Bay, 6.5 miles northeast of Seldovia. Cook Inlet has 8 of Alaska's 10 species of harvested trees . . . though most are not in commercial quantities. Sitka spruce is the most valuable species in the Cook Inlet region. (Rick Furniss)

Right — An aerial view of Seldovia, population 612, a Kachemak Bay town relying on fishing, fish processing, logging and, to a lesser extent, tourism. Seldovia has a rather mild climate, with a year-round average temperature of about 39, and annual precipitation of 28 inches. Connected to the rest of the world only by air or state ferry, the town has retained much of its "old Alaskan" charm, although development of Lower Cook Inlet oil and gas fields, along with increased tourism, could trigger considerable changes in the future. (Jim Rearden, Staff)

Far right — Salmon eggs are processed in a cannery near Seldovia before shipment to markets in the Far East. (Rick Furniss)

Below — Ice clogs the Homer small-boat harbor in early spring. (Jim Rearden, Staff)

Right — Homer, second-largest community on the Kenai Peninsula (with 1,538 in town and 4,000 in the area), is on the north shore of Kachemak Bay, 125 air miles southwest of Anchorage. As the photo suggests, Homer is in a spectacular location — with its view of the Kenai Mountains across the bay, the town is called the "Shangri-la of Alaska." The town was established in 1895 on Homer Spit, which arcs several miles out into the bay, and named for a prospector, Homer Pennock. The coal mining company for which Pennock worked built one of Alaska's first railroads on the spit at the turn of the century, and continued to ship coal from the area until the Second World War. In the early 1920's several families of fishermen settled in Homer and their success with garden vegetables aroused the interest of homesteaders. Today, the once-isolated community is humming — tourism increases each year, the town's fishing industry remains as an important part of the economy, and there is the possibility of future oil-industry impact with exploratory drilling in Lower Cook Inlet . . . a mixed blessing, some would say. (Rick Furniss)

Left — A tour boat passes Gull Island, in Kachemak Bay. (Neil and Betty Johannsen)
Below — Crab feast at a wilderness lodge in China Poot Bay, on the east shore of Kachemak Bay, 9 miles southeast of Homer. (Nancy Simmerman)
Lower left — Butter clams are roasted along the shore of Kachemak Bay, one of Alaska's richest bodies of water in terms of marine life. (Nancy Simmerman)
Right — Riding high at an informal rodeo at the ranch of Stanley Jones, 20 miles east of Homer. Another local happening, the Homer Winter Carnival, is usually held the first weekend in February. (Jim Rearden, Staff)

Above — Fishing is big business in Lower Cook Inlet. Here a boat heads out into Kachemak Bay, leaving Homer Spit behind. (Jim Rearden, Staff)
Right — Icing fish at a processing plant in Homer. (Dan Kowalski)
Far right — Loading a salmon tender with fish caught by a salmon drift gill-net boat in Cook Inlet. (Jim Rearden, Staff)

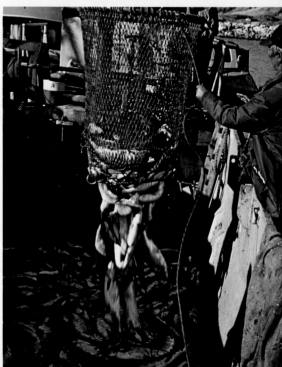

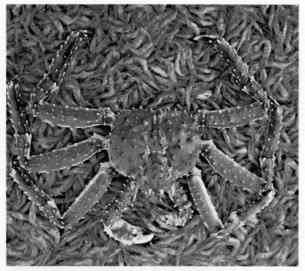

Far left — Pat Brown, crew member aboard the Homer-based shrimp trawler *Columbian,* pulls the trip cord to dump shrimp from the trawl into the vessel's deck bin. Shellfish — pink shrimp, spot shrimp and coon-striped shrimp; tanner crab, king crab and Dungeness crab, primarily — are important resources in Lower Cook Inlet. For shrimp-identification photo, see page 139. (Jim Rearden, Staff)

Above — A king crab in the shrimp trawl. (Rick Furniss)

Left — Frozen blocks of peeled shrimp, ready for market in a Homer seafood-processing plant. (Jim Rearden, Staff)

Left — The village of Ninilchik, 38 miles southwest of Kenai, looks across Cook Inlet at Redoubt Volcano. Photo was taken in early spring. (Rick Furniss)

Lower left — Fish boats at Ninilchik; the settlement also relies to a small extent on agriculture, and formerly was involved in fur farming. Ninilchik, with a population of about 134, was first settled by employees of the Russian-American Company. (Dan Kowalski)

Below — A plea from villagers. (Dan Kowalski)

Right — Ninilchik is a favorite subject for photographers — perhaps second-fiddle to Turnagain Arm and Kachemak Bay, but definitely near the top. The Russian Orthodox church, Redoubt Volcano and a sunset over Cook Inlet . . . how could we resist? (Stephen Hilson)

Left — Strolling the beach at Clam Gulch. (Tom Walker)

Lower left — Prized are Cook Inlet's razor clams, which despite heavy digging appear to be growing larger each season. Other species include cockles, surf clams, butter clams, Pacific littlenecks and horse clams — taken mostly from the Kachemak Bay region. (Helen Rhode, reprinted from *The MILEPOST®*)

Below — With the first minus tides of spring, thousands of clam-crazy Cook Inletters swarm to the beaches along the eastern shore, primarily south of Kenai River to Kachemak Bay. Others take boats or small planes across Cook Inlet to the clam-rich beaches near Polly Creek. (Mark Kelley, reprinted from *ALASKA®* magazine)

Opposite page — Near Anchor Point, northwest of Homer, is the village of Nikolaevsk, founded 10 years ago by expatriate Russian "Old Believers," whose ancestors refused to accept reforms of the rites of Russian Orthodoxy introduced in the 1650's. The villagers rely on fishing and construction work, and have started a boatbuilding business. Victor and Maria Yakunin were photographed with their daughter Olga, the day of a mass naturalization ceremony. After the ceremony the new United States citizens pledged allegiance to the flag for the first time. (Both photos by Jim Rearden, Staff, reprinted from *ALASKA®* magazine)

North Kenai

The North Kenai area, with the peninsula's largest town (Kenai), is many things . . . the oil capital of Cook Inlet, and a tremendous land of rivers and lakes in the Kenai National Moose Range and the Chugach National Forest, two huge set-asides that dominate the region. For purposes of this discussion, North Kenai extends from the southern boundary of the Moose Range to the shores of Turnagain Arm, with its eastern border roughly following the crest of the Kenai Mountains.

Left — Kenai Lake, not often this calm, extends southwest 24 miles from the head of Kenai River to the mouth of Snow River, 22 miles northwest of Seward. (John Wenger)

Below — Four oil rigs in Cook Inlet . . . out of the 14 that are operating in the upper inlet. Pipelines carry oil and gas to shoreline plants and loading docks; some gas is used in Alaska, most is shipped south. A petrochemical complex north of Kenai ships fertilizer and LNG — liquefied natural gas — to Japan. (Nancy Simmerman)

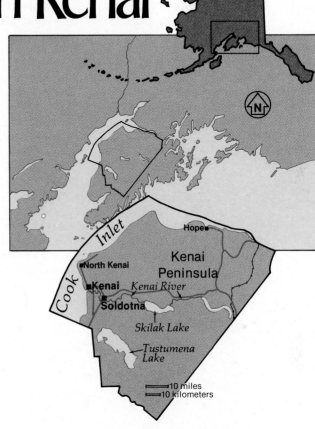

Right — Fort Saint Nicholas, built by Grigor Konovalov in 1791, was the second permanent Russian settlement in Alaska. This church, long out of use, is one of several attractions in the Kenai area. (Jim Thiele)
Below — Kenai, population 5,223, is at the mouth of Kenai River, 65 miles southwest of Anchorage. Twelve miles upriver is Soldotna, a rapidly growing community of about 1,275 established in the 1940's because of its location at the junction of the Sterling Highway and Kenai Spur Road.
(Betty Johannsen, Staff)
Lower right — Corner detail on the old church at Fort Saint Nicholas. (Nancy Simmerman)
Far Right — Light planes and passengers on an unnamed glacier high in the Kenai Mountains. Bush pilots in Kenai, Homer and other Kenai Peninsula towns provide easy access to the back country, although many visitors fly directly from Anchorage. (Nancy Simmerman)

40

Far left — Gas is flared from one of Cook Inlet's oil rigs. (Brian Springer)
Left — Helicopters provide quick access to offshore oil rigs in Cook Inlet. The rigs also are serviced by rig-tender boats — most based in the Kenai area. (Anthony Flora)
Below — A Cook Inlet rig tender battles to stay alongside in a stiff tide. (Nancy Simmerman)
Right — An escape module from a Mobil Oil platform undergoes its annual test. Accidental dunkings in Cook Inlet are to be avoided at all costs — the currents are swift and the waters cold. (Anthony Flora)

Left — The Collier Carbon and Chemical plant, north of Kenai, produces ammonia and urea for fertilizer. This time exposure was taken one night in March. (Rick Furniss)

Above — Oil refineries along North Kenai Road. The Phillips LNG plant ships liquefied gas to Japan; Tesoro and Standard Oil refineries each ship thousands of barrels of gas and oil to western seaports. (Nancy Simmerman)

Above right — A tanker berthed at the North Kenai offshore-loading terminal. (Nancy Simmerman)

45

Far left — The Kenai National Moose Range, with headquarters in Kenai (one block east of Fort Kenay), offers 1.7 million acres of land, lakes and rivers — mostly wilderness. The range was established in 1941 and has become a popular area for hikers, hunters, sport fishermen, cross-country skiers, canoeists, kayakers, snowshoers, berry pickers, photographers . . . most everybody, it seems. (Nancy Simmerman)

Left — A kayaker on one of the many rivers in the Moose Range. (Nancy Simmerman)

Lower left — A moose and calf. The Kenai Peninsula subspecies was at one time thought to be the largest of Alaska's moose — largest of all moose. Kenai National Moose Range also is populated by Dall sheep, mountain goats, black bear, grizzly bear, wolves, beaver, mink and numerous other mammals. (Gary M. Brown, reprinted from *The MILEPOST®*)

Left — Hope, population about 50, is on the shore of Turnagain Arm in northeastern Kenai Peninsula, at the end of a 16.5-mile gravel road. This historic mining community was founded in 1896 by gold seekers who were actively working Resurrection Creek and its tributary streams. Many residents enjoy the relative seclusion, and hope that their settlement — already becoming a popular weekend destination for visitors from the Anchorage area — will not be overrun. About 9 miles from Hope is the site of another former gold-mining boom town, Sunrise. Don't bother looking for the town, though — nothing is left. (C & J Peck)

Lower left — Skiers from Anchorage get off of an Alaska Railroad train at Grandview, north Kenai Peninsula. (Nancy Simmerman)

Right — Turnagain Pass, elevation 988 feet, is a favorite winter-sports area for Cook Inletters. Snowshoeing, cross-country skiing and snowmobiling are winter activities; in summer the area is loaded with hikers and wild flowers. (Nancy Simmerman)

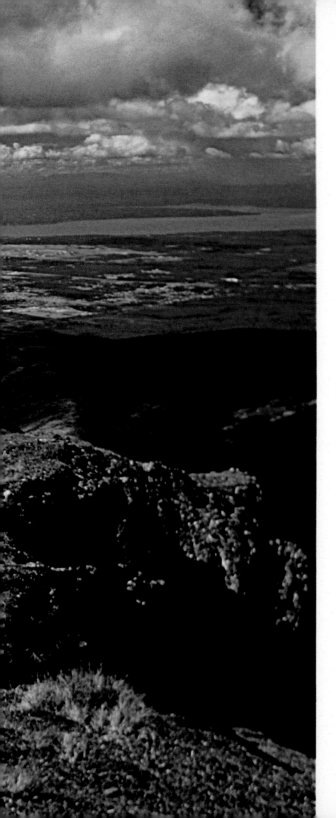

Greater Greater Anchorage

Including the Anchorage Municipality and its neighbors along Knik Arm and Turnagain Arm, as well as the wilderness at Anchorage's back door.

There isn't really a place called Greater-Greater Anchorage — that's just a descriptive term for most everything in the vicinity of the huge Anchorage Municipality, population about 200,000 and growing geometrically. Our Greater-Greater Anchorage territory begins near the muddy head of 48-mile-long Turnagain Arm, southeast of Anchorage, and follows the Seward Highway into Anchorage proper. From there we head northeast along Knik Arm for 40 miles to the mouths of the Knik and Matanuska rivers; then into the Chugach Mountains, encircling Chugach State Park as we complete the triangle at Portage Glacier. *Left* — An overview of Anchorage from the Chugach Mountains. At the far left is Turnagain Arm; Mount Susitna ("The Sleeping Lady") is in the center, and Knik Arm is to the right. (Neil and Betty Johannsen)

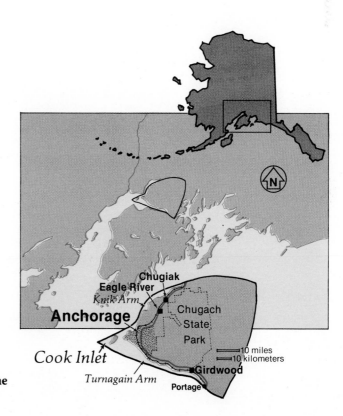

Far left — **Dawn over iceberg-filled Portage Lake, at the terminus of Portage Glacier in the Chugach Mountains, between Turnagain Arm and Prince William Sound. Portage and Burns glaciers are in the background. The surrounding recreation area, 53 miles southeast of Anchorage, offers three campgrounds, a lodge and several hiking trails. (Nancy Simmerman)**

Left — **Hoarfrost builds up on trees and shrubs in the Portage area during the winter. (Nancy Simmerman)**

Below — **The Alaska Railroad offers service from Anchorage along Turnagain Arm to Portage, and by shuttle run from Portage through two tunnels to Whittier, on the Prince William Sound side of Portage Pass. Although Whittier is only a few miles southwest of Portage, it falls outside of the Cook Inlet drainage and is not covered in this edition; for details on Whittier, see the "Prince William Sound" issue of** *ALASKA GEOGRAPHIC®* **, Volume 2, Number 3. (Nancy Simmerman)**

Only 40 miles southeast of downtown Anchorage is the Girdwood-Mount Alyeska recreation area, a favorite spot for Cook Inletters summer and winter.

Far left — Alyeska Resort, with snow from November to May, offers spectacular chairlift rides three-fourths of the way to the top of 3,939-foot Mount Alyeska. In the background is Turnagain Arm; also visible is the Seward Highway. (Susan Hackley Johnson)

Left — The same chairlifts whisk visitors to the top for spectacular summer views of the area. (Gary Brown)

Lower left — Another snowy day in Girdwood. (Nancy Simmerman)

Below — The Alyeska area also offers Erickson's Crow Creek Mine, where visitors can pan for gold in an 1898 mining camp. (Nancy Simmerman)

Some of the many moods of Turnagain Arm, a narrow inlet that almost makes the Kenai Peninsula Kenai Island.

Far left — Windblown snow over the arm's frozen salt-ice in March. (Nancy Simmerman)

Left — The famous Turnagain Arm tidal bore, produced by onrushing tides that can rise 30 feet in 6 hours, is easily observed from turnouts along the Seward Highway southeast of Anchorage. Good viewpoints are 32.6 and 36.5 miles from town. (Nancy Simmerman)

Below — Patterns in the Turnagain Arm mud flats. (Tim Thompson)

Birds of varying descriptions are seen along the Seward Highway southeast of Anchorage.

Above and left — One of the area's "institutions" is the Bird House Bar, a rough-hewn little place at Bird Creek, 25 miles from Anchorage. (Sharon Paul, Staff)

Right — Potter Marsh, just southeast of Anchorage, is a favorite bird-watching spot. (Tim Thompson)

Far right — Canada geese, photographed at Potter Marsh in spring. (Nancy Simmerman)

Anchorage is growing rapidly, as these photos demonstrate. Today's population — anybody's guess, really — is about 200,000. Some say the figure could hit 300,000 by 1980 if certain developments proceed (exploitation of Lower Cook Inlet oil and gas fields; construction of a new state capital near Willow; building of a proposed gas pipeline from the North Slope to markets in the Lower 48; development of outer continental shelf petroleum reserves, and so forth).
Left — Aerial view of Anchorage taken in September 1977, showing the latest high-rise buildings under construction.
(Betty Johannsen, Staff)
Below — Downtown Anchorage and Knik Arm ice, photographed in the winter of 1975-76. Note additional buildings in photo at left. (Rick Furniss)

Anchorage began in 1913 as a temporary tent city during construction of the Alaska Central Railway, later to become The Alaska Railroad. At right is the tent town, with limbs cut off many trees for firewood. (George Harrington Collection, Courtesy of the Alaska Historical Library) Lower three photos on this page show stock in the original railway, and scenes during the construction period. (Courtesy of The Alaska Railroad)

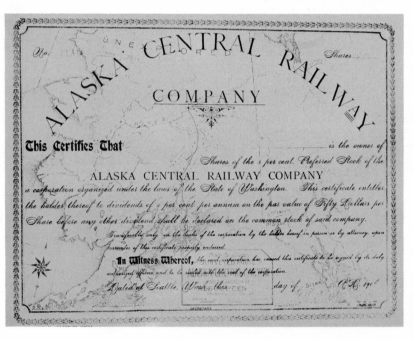

Anchorage was first known as Woodrow and Ship Creek. The enduring name, chosen because Ship Creek offered a decent anchorage for incoming vessels, was adopted in 1914 when a post office was established. Photos on this page (all courtesy of The Alaska Railroad) depict scenes in the bustling little town, including an important land auction in 1915. Population of Anchorage was 6,000 by 1917, 1,856 in 1920 (after construction of the railroad), 11,254 in 1950 and 44,237 in 1970.

The growth of Anchorage is difficult to comprehend, in some respects. The town has long been a bustling, active place, but expansion in recent "pipeline years" has been unparalleled. The city's growth leveled to some extent in late 1977, and is expected to remain in a relatively stable position through mid-1978, but who knows after that? *Left* — Downtown at dusk in February, with the Chugach Mountains as a backdrop. (Neil and Betty Johannsen) *Right* — Star, Anchorage's celebrity reindeer, hitched at a downtown parking meter. When the city threatened to evict Star from her home in a downtown yard, irked residents came to the defense. Star stayed. (Lael Morgan, Staff) *Lower right* — The Financial Plaza, one of many recent additions to the Anchorage skyline. (Neil and Betty Johannsen) *Far Right* — Fourth Avenue at night. (Marty Loken, Staff)

Additional signs of the times in the Anchorage area . . .
Far left — A preserved log cabin (the visitor information center) contrasts against one of the city's high-rise hotels. (Lael Morgan, Staff)
Left — A potlatch in Anchorage, sponsored by the Cook Inlet Native Association. (Lael Morgan, Staff)
Lower left — Anchorage is becoming a major cultural center of the North. In this case, the cultural event is a performance of "Macbeth" at Alaska Methodist University. (Marty Loken, Staff)
Above and right — Signs of Japanese tourism and business are noticed throughout Anchorage. (Lael Morgan and Marty Loken, Staff)

67

Street and highway construction goes on . . . and on . . . in the Anchorage area.
Below — A flagperson in downtown Anchorage traffic. (Marty Loken, Staff)
Right — Aerial view of the Seward Highway, heading south from Anchorage toward the Kenai Peninsula; photographed in March 1977. (George Herben)
Far right — Another major artery, Minnesota Drive, carries traffic by Westchester Lagoon in the downtown area. (Betty Johannsen, Staff)

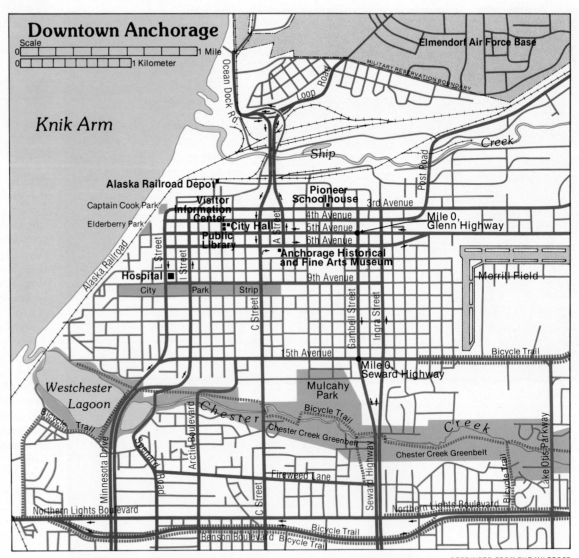

REPRINTED FROM THE MILEPOST

68

Left — Aerial view of some Anchorage institutions. From lower left to upper right: Alaska Methodist University, Providence Hospital, Alaska Psychiatric Institute and a portion of the University of Alaska, Anchorage, campus. Several new facilities have been added since this photo was taken. (Nancy Simmerman)

Above — Wintertime in Anchorage, where snowfall averages 60 inches a year and the average temperature — in January, the coldest month — is 13° above. (George Herben)

Below — In spring and summer some Anchorage streets tend to become muddy and dusty. (Marty Loken, Staff)

Left — Typical modern housing in the Anchorage area. This neighborhood surrounds Lake Otis; in the background is a portion of the University of Alaska, Anchorage, campus. (Nancy Simmerman)
Lower left — In winter many residents get around on cross-country skis — in this case by skiing beside Chester Creek over a trail that is used for bicycles in the summer. (John and Margaret Ibbotson)
Below — Mobile homes have become an important source of housing in the Anchorage area. This group is in "roundup" formation; in the foreground is the new Alaska Hospital. (Betty Johannsen, Staff)

Far left — Interconnected Lakes Hood and Spenard, just north of Anchorage International Airport, house more small aircraft than any air base in the world — including many of Anchorage's 50 air-taxi companies. In the winter many small planes shift to skis from floats or wheels. (Rick Furniss)

Above — British Airways and Air France are two of more than a dozen major air carriers landing at Anchorage International Airport. Other foreign carriers include Japan Air Lines, KLM Royal Dutch Airlines, Lufthansa German Airlines, Sabena Belgian World Airlines, Scandinavian Airlines System and Korean Airlines. (Nancy Simmerman)

Left — Major domestic air carriers include Alaska Airlines, Wien Air Alaska, Northwest Orient Airlines, Western Airlines. (Nancy Simmerman)

Right — Lake Hood is ringed with float-equipped planes in the summer. (Marty Loken, Staff)

73

Shipping is another important activity in Anchorage, transportation hub of Alaska. *Below* — Japanese imports bound for showrooms and car lots throughout Southcentral and Interior Alaska await distribution at the Port of Anchorage. (Marty Loken, Staff) *Right* — A Sea-Land ship at the Port of Anchorage. Also sending ships to Anchorage from the Northwest is TOTE — Totem Ocean Trailer Express. (Neil and Betty Johannsen) *Far right* — Ice fog drops over a ship at the Port of Anchorage. Negotiating Cook Inlet can be tricky in the winter because of ferocious tides, fog and the inlet's churning ice floes. (Neil and Betty Johannsen)

The Alaska Railroad provides a link to the Interior (with runs from Anchorage to Fairbanks, via Mount McKinley National Park), and to Prince William Sound and the Kenai Peninsula (with routes ending in Whittier and Seward). *Far left* — Head-on view of an Alaska Railroad engine preparing to depart Anchorage for Fairbanks — a daily trip from late May to early September. (Marty Loken, Staff) *Upper left* — Passengers headed for Anchorage from the Interior enjoy the domeliner car. (Lael Morgan, Staff) *Lower left* — Fireman Ken Smith, left, and engineer Pete Fleming aboard one of The Alaska Railroad engines. (Lael Morgan, Staff)

Right — An Anchorage cannery worker checks herring on their way to the grinder — last stop after removal of herring roe for shipment to Japan. (Marty Loken, Staff) *Upper right* — Generators at the Eklutna power plant, a hydroelectric plant northeast of Anchorage, supply some of the city's power, but a larger share comes from the Beluga gas fields across Knik Arm. (Marty Loken, Staff) *Lower right* — Modern communications have come to Alaska, with Anchorage as a central switchboard. Elizabeth McMorrow learns how to use long-distance equipment at RCA Alaska. (Marty Loken, Staff)

Left — Biggest wintertime celebration in the North is the annual Anchorage Fur Rendezvous (February 10-19, 1978), which each season attracts more than 10,000 out-of-town visitors. The festival began in 1936 as a fur auction, where trappers could bring their pelts to town and make a few extra dollars selling them directly to buyers from around the world, thus cutting out the middlemen. The fur auction still is held, but the celebration also involves sled-dog races, a folk-dance festival, ice hockey, a curling bonspiel, basketball, wrestling, auto races on ice, beard-growing contest, the Miners' and Trappers' Ball and half a dozen other events. (Neil and Betty Johannsen)

Right — Anchorage has several enclosed public swimming pools . . . for those who would rather get their exercise indoors during the long winter months. This pool is at West High School. (Marty Loken, Staff)

Lower right — Helicopter skiing is an exciting outdoor sport available in the Anchorage area. These skiers are in the Chugach Mountains, southeast of Anchorage. (Nancy Simmerman)

Far right — Big event of the Fur Rendezvous is the World Championship Sled Dog Race, held over a three-day period. (Neil and Betty Johannsen)

Additional recreational activities in the Anchorage area . . .

Left — Hooligan (eulachon) dipping at Twentymile River, which flows into Turnagain Arm 46 miles southeast of Anchorage. Fishing for hooligans is best in May; silver salmon may be taken from this river in August and September. (Nancy Simmerman)

Above — Baseball is popular everywhere, of course, but perhaps even more so in Alaska. The count was 3-and-2, 1 out, in this junior-high game. (Marty Loken, Staff)

Right — Campbell Creek is the site of a wet and wacky raft competition each year. (Jean Petersen)

Upper right — Weekend camping "Alaska style" can involve a bush-plane flight to a remote Cook Inlet beach. This couple flew from Anchorage to Kachemak Bay, on the Kenai Peninsula. (Rick Furniss)

Above — Surfsailors, conventional sailboats and swimmers share Jewel Lake on a hot summer day in Anchorage. (Neil and Betty Johannsen)

Chugach State Park, largest in the system with 495,204 acres, surrounds the backside of Anchorage. The park is accessible from several different points, including the Seward Highway and Glenn Highway, and offers 91 camping units and 62 picnic spaces.
Left — A view of the Chugach Mountains, in Chugach State Park, from Abbott Road in Anchorage. (John and Margaret Ibbotson)
Below — A weary hiker at the top of Wolverine Peak, 4,455 feet, southeast of Anchorage in Chugach State Park. (Neil and Betty Johannsen)
Right — Eagle River Valley is one of several access points to Chugach State Park. (Neil and Betty Johannsen)

"Horoscopes," Carolyn Torkko tells her astrology classes at Anchorage Community College, "are the directions that come with every baby."

Curious about the future of Anchorage, we asked Ms. Torkko, a professional astrologer, to cast a horoscope for the state's largest city. Here are a few of her findings:

• Anchorage develops by crisis and upheaval. The massing of power in the sign Cancer is a most forceful, energizing, invigorating, disruptive combination. Visionary ideals clash with conservative realities. Events seem to crowd in on the area and it must react as best it can in emergency situations. (The sign Cancer emerges from the date of the first land auction in town — 2 P.M. on July 10, 1915.)

• Since the capital couldn't come to Anchorage, Anchorage will, crablike, extend its claws around the center of government, enfolding it in suburban sprawl.

• Anchorage is slightly schizophrenic. On one hand the pull is toward the progressive and innovative in legislation, legal precedents and general concern for people; conversely, the timid, self-protective, conservative instincts of the sign Cancer tend to regard innovation with suspicion.

• Astrologically speaking, the area had a progressed New Moon in 1976, an occurrence that happens only once every 20 to 30 years. This means the beginning of a new cycle of development that will culminate shortly after the turn of the century.

• Plans and proposals for some form of transportation across Knik Arm will be likely to generate much energy and controversy next year, from March through October.

• The Anchorage area is particularly susceptible to earthquakes in 1977 and 1978. □

And, speaking of the future . . .

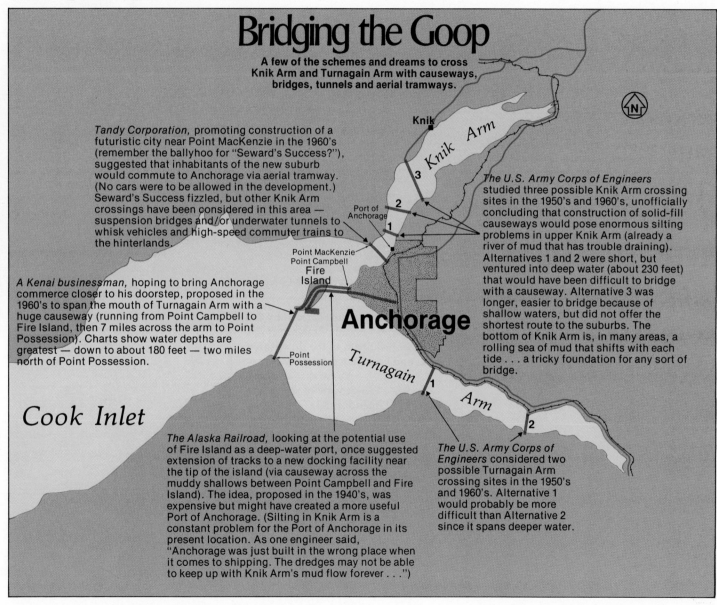

Bridging the Goop

A few of the schemes and dreams to cross Knik Arm and Turnagain Arm with causeways, bridges, tunnels and aerial tramways.

Tandy Corporation, promoting construction of a futuristic city near Point MacKenzie in the 1960's (remember the ballyhoo for "Seward's Success?"), suggested that inhabitants of the new suburb would commute to Anchorage via aerial tramway. (No cars were to be allowed in the development.) Seward's Success fizzled, but other Knik Arm crossings have been considered in this area — suspension bridges and/or underwater tunnels to whisk vehicles and high-speed commuter trains to the hinterlands.

A Kenai businessman, hoping to bring Anchorage commerce closer to his doorstep, proposed in the 1960's to span the mouth of Turnagain Arm with a huge causeway (running from Point Campbell to Fire Island, then 7 miles across the arm to Point Possession). Charts show water depths are greatest — down to about 180 feet — two miles north of Point Possession.

The U.S. Army Corps of Engineers studied three possible Knik Arm crossing sites in the 1950's and 1960's, unofficially concluding that construction of solid-fill causeways would pose enormous silting problems in upper Knik Arm (already a river of mud that has trouble draining). Alternatives 1 and 2 were short, but ventured into deep water (about 230 feet) that would have been difficult to bridge with a causeway. Alternative 3 was longer, easier to bridge because of shallow waters, but did not offer the shortest route to the suburbs. The bottom of Knik Arm is, in many areas, a rolling sea of mud that shifts with each tide . . . a tricky foundation for any sort of bridge.

The Alaska Railroad, looking at the potential use of Fire Island as a deep-water port, once suggested extension of tracks to a new docking facility near the tip of the island (via causeway across the muddy shallows between Point Campbell and Fire Island). The idea, proposed in the 1940's, was expensive but might have created a more useful Port of Anchorage. (Silting in Knik Arm is a constant problem for the Port of Anchorage in its present location. As one engineer said, "Anchorage was just built in the wrong place when it comes to shipping. The dredges may not be able to keep up with Knik Arm's mud flow forever . . .")

The U.S. Army Corps of Engineers considered two possible Turnagain Arm crossing sites in the 1950's and 1960's. Alternative 1 would probably be more difficult than Alternative 2 since it spans deeper water.

Knik

Knik Arm

Port of Anchorage

Point MacKenzie

Point Campbell

Fire Island

Anchorage

Point Possession

Turnagain Arm

Cook Inlet

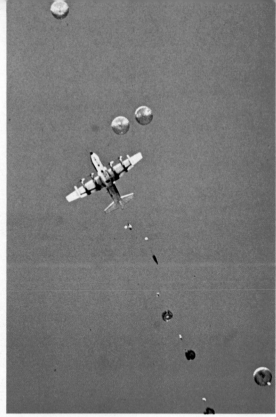

Anchorage is also surrounded by the
military — mainly Elmendorf Air
Force Base, just north of the downtown
area, and Fort Richardson, an Army
base east of town.
Above — **Aerial view of sprawling
Elmendorf Air Force Base.
(U.S. Air Force)**
Upper right — **A practice drop from
aircraft based at Elmendorf.
(U.S. Air Force)**
Right — **A planning room of the
Tactical Fighter Squadron at
Elmendorf. (U.S. Air Force)**

The Good Friday earthquake of March 27, 1964, dramatically changed the face of Anchorage and other towns in Southcentral Alaska. The quake caused millions of dollars in damage, but also gave the downtown area a new financial incentive to repair and restore. Government relief funds, in the form of SBA loans, were offered to those who wished to rebuild. Most did, and a distinctly new Anchorage began to emerge.

Upper left — The home of Lowell Thomas Jr., after the quake hit the Turnagain residential area, totally destroying the neighborhood. (Gil Mull)

Left — The west end of the Turnagain area, now designated Earthquake Park, still bears scars of the 1964 quake. Note folds in the land where mounds of earth were tossed up like high ocean waves. (Rick Furniss)

Above — Fourth Avenue on March 27, 1964, shortly after the quake struck. (Gil Mull)

Left — About 26 miles northeast of downtown Anchorage is the Tanaina Indian village of Eklutna, with its historic Russian Orthodox church and burial houses. (Tee Balog)

Below — Knik Arm, north of Anchorage, is a 40-mile-long muddy inlet. Knik River and Matanuska River flow into the head of the arm, a popular waterfowl-hunting area. This view is from the west side of lower Knik Arm, looking north. (John and Margaret Ibbotson)

Right — Looking across Knik Arm toward Anchorage in early January. (Neil and Betty Johannsen)

THE PEOPLE OF COOK INLET

By Lael Morgan, Associate Editor,
ALASKA® *magazine*

Above — **A crowd at the World Championship Sled Dog Race, held in mid-February during the Fur Rendezvous.** (Lael Morgan, Staff)
Right — **Edith Bullock, Anchorage businesswoman who taught at Nome, ran a tug and barge firm in Kotzebue, served as a legislator and, at one point, was named "Man of the Year" by the Anchorage Chamber of Commerce.** (Lael Morgan, Staff)

Most editions of *ALASKA GEOGRAPHIC®* deal heavily with forests and tundra, but for Cook Inlet we must consider a new arena — the city. Over half the population of the nation's largest state is crowded into the U-shaped parcel of land between the Chugach Mountains and Captain Cook's famous stretch of ocean, and people have long since outdistanced the wild game in number and importance.

Usually they settle here for two reasons: they come to get something (jobs, money, fresh air, a crack at the last frontier) or to get away from something (the law, the mother-in-law, the pressures of the outside world). And in a few hundred thousand cases to date, people must have found what they wanted.

"You either like it or you don't," maintains Walter Hickel, pioneer Anchorage developer who later became governor and then U.S. Secretary of the Interior. "If you like it, you stay. If you don't, you bitch. If you bitch, you leave."

Those who elect to stay are unique — a marvelous collection of mavericks, dreamers, nuts and utter damn fools unmatched anywhere in the world. And, in assessing them, you must throw away standard criteria.

"I think things here have to be scaled to match the size of the country," Hickel says. And so it is that the philosophy of the area is summed up on the bumper sticker: WE DON'T GIVE A DAMN HOW THEY DO IT OUTSIDE.

You can't tell the people who wield power in Anchorage by their school ties. Some of them never went to school and more than a few don't own ties. Nurses at local hospitals will tell you a number of apparently down-and-out sidewalk drunks land in Anchorage emergency rooms with rolls of $100 bills in their pockets, while in the posh sections of town — Geneva Woods or Turnagain — it is not unusual for an upper-crust citizen to trade in his registered Irish Setter and his Lincoln to help settle a fuel bill.

The area claims one of the highest percentages of college graduates in the United States including — likely as not — your office janitor and the local garbage collector. Wally Hickel, who arrived here with 37 cents in his pocket in 1940, got his start washing dishes, while another former governor, Bill Egan, used to muscle freight out of airplanes for a living.

Mrs. Evangeline Atwood, leading Anchorage socialite, served as a social worker during the Depression and is proud of it. Colonel Marvin R. "Muktuk" Marston, who established the Eskimo National Guard and later made it big in real estate, is remembered by early settlers as "that man who used to peddle fish downtown at $1 a pound."

Many of the area's leading citizens have gone through bankruptcy — some more than once — and some have been in jail. In more conservative communities either could mark a person for life, but in Anchorage you are judged by what you're doing now and what you plan to do. When a town has its eye on the future, there's not much time for the backward glance.

A couple summers ago, Hollywood movie actor Steve McQueen was cited by local police for drag-racing on the main street and, in a disgruntled parting shot, he called Anchorage a "hick town." Yet because it is a major fueling stop for international over-the-pole flights, Anchorage attracts some top talent — major ballet troops, movie stars, recording artists, kings, queens and presidents. It is a stop for 10 international airlines, which means it's possible to dine here every night of the week with someone who speaks a different language. It is also possible to drive to Anchorage International Airport in the morning and have supper in Tokyo, London or Copenhagen.

Left — **Bob and Evangeline Atwood, publishers of the** *Anchorage Times,* **Alaska's heftiest newspaper. Atwood's best editorial was probably written immediately after the 1964 Alaska earthquake — a stirring piece that, according to some, set the spirit for recovery in Southcentral. When the quake started Atwood was sitting at home playing his trumpet. The couple lost their house and many of its contents, but Atwood joked in print the next day that a sour note must have started everything shaking. (Lael Morgan, Staff)**

Left — **Reporter Howard Weaver, right, one of several partners in the lively** *Alaska Advocate,* **joins other staffers in mailing the latest edition. (Lael Morgan, Staff)**
Above — **Miriam Florez, owner of Anchorage's smallest restaurant, Taco Florez, came north to Alaska from New York City and Colombia, South America. Miriam's little van-eatery is only 9 feet long, 4 feet wide and 4 feet tall. (Marty Loken, Staff)**

Above — **Orville Lake, veteran Anchorage dog musher, with his fox-skin cap at the Anchorage Fur Rendezvous. (Lael Morgan, Staff)**
Right — **Nellie Brown, the first white woman in Anchorage, now lives in the Pioneers' Home at Palmer. (Lael Morgan, Staff)**
Lower right — **A few members of the Han family, recent immigrants to Alaska from Korea, in their small Government Hill restaurant. Han says he was looking for a place where a man could find rewards for hard work — and Anchorage is apparently the place. (Lael Morgan, Staff)**

And there are international colonies here. There are strong Japanese, Chinese, Filipino and Korean communities, Vietnamese, a vocal black population and some 10,000 urbanized Alaskan Eskimos and Indians.

You can buy anything you want in Anchorage — a Paris gown, fresh oysters, muktuk, black market polar bear skins, cocaine or papayas.

It's no big thing to drop $200 for two at a top Anchorage restaurant, breakfast the next morning at McDonald's and join the old boys at the Union Club for lunch and a game of panguingue.

As for the people — take a cross section starting early one morning at Top of the World, a first-class restaurant on the top floor of the Anchorage Westward hotel. Stewards Ruben Luna, lately of the Dominican Republic, and Ken Millard, a Southerner, have just wrapped up the night shift and are taking a break to enjoy a royal view. To the east, the snow-covered Chugach Range blushes with the early sun. Below, a thousand Anchorage chimneys carry fat plumes of smoke and in the west the inlet shimmers with ice-based mist.

"You should have been with us Christmas Eve," they tell the visiting photographer. "That night the northern lights were absolutely wild and we toasted them with a glass of champagne."

Across Ship Creek Yumi and Henry Han are just opening up their small, viewless Korean restaurant on Government Hill. Since they immigrated here two years ago they have worked seven days a week, from 10 A.M. till 10 P.M., but remain enthusiastic about their chosen spot. They came, Henry says, because they were looking for a place where a man who was willing to work could really work. And this is the right place, not to mention the fishing. "In the summer," he says, "we take off after work and really enjoy that."

Another early morning riser is M. M. "Moose" Moore,

92

former guide and state legislator, who opened the Health Club at the Captain Cook Hotel in 1965. He came to Anchorage in 1946, picked up his nickname by backpacking terrible loads of moose rather than leave meat behind, and is today in better shape than men half his age. Like many other Anchorageites, he owns a condominium in Hawaii and regularly threatens to retire there, but there's something about this country. . . .

Rosita B. Decastellanos immigrated here from Russia in 1964 accompanied by international headlines. An Alaskan tourist had fallen in love with her and refused to leave U.S.S.R. without her, although his visa expired. Khrushchev himself signed her final papers and, although her Alaskan marriage didn't last (she later married a man she met while serving as interpreter for the Mexican Olympics), her enthusiasm for this area is still strong. Early on, she opened a dress shop in Fairbanks, branched into Anchorage and now bases here full time.

"It's hard to do business in this big city," she admits. "Lots of sharks here in town." But she wouldn't consider moving. She likes the business climate and the handy international airport.

Famed bush pilot Bob Reeve came here in 1932, after flying in South America, and recalls the park strip, near downtown, was the original airport.

"Everyone in the city turned out to clear the brush for Merrill Field . . . very civic minded. And the airport manager was also the local butcher."

Having made up his mind early to "beat the odds," Reeve parlayed surplus airplanes into highly successful Reeve Aleutian Airways, logged some 8,000 flying hours over the world's roughest country and also survived the Anchorage earthquake of 1964, swinging and swaying at the top of the Anchorage Westward, where he happened to be having a birthday party. (Last year he celebrated his 76th birthday, and, although he was suffering from a bad

Above — **Folk dancers whoop it up at Bird Creek, south of Anchorage.** (Nancy Simmerman)
Left — **Myrtle Stolnaser, owner of Club 25, in one of Anchorage's oldest buildings. See page 16 for a photograph of Club 25 and its surroundings.** (Lael Morgan, Staff)

93

Lucy Cuddy, who pioneered as a teacher and is now chief executive of the First National Bank of Anchorage.
(Lael Morgan, Staff)

back, there was a bright spot. "At 76 I'm recovering on workman's compensation for an on-the-job accident," he notes.)

Despite urban sprawl, the excitement of frontier living still lingers in Anchorage, not only for bush pilots but for the average Joe who, with an hour's drive or short bush flight, can land himself in some delightfully primitive country for hunting, fishing, cross-country skiing, mountain climbing or hang gliding.

Moose still appear routinely in Anchorage backyards and the main dog-sled racing trails are within the city limits. Plenty of bright lights for those who require them and some marvelous options for those who don't.

Naturally, these options attract a great variety of people — boomers, hustlers, homesteaders, trappers, white-collar professionals, academians, artists, some of the sharpest Native leaders in the state, politicians, little old ladies in tennis shoes and future champion Olympic skiers — and that's the combination that makes Cook Inlet exciting.

It's summed up best, perhaps, by Lucy Cuddy, chairman of the board of the First National Bank of Anchorage, who pioneered as a teacher when there were only 35,000 whites and 35,000 Natives in the entire territory:

"What's so fascinating about it is that everyone came here from somewhere else. Everyone has a little something different, and there were — and still are — so few of us, which makes everyone more important." □

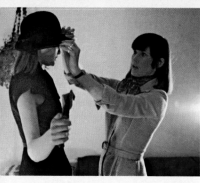

Above — City Hall at 9 A.M.; Anchorage Mayor George Sullivan and his office staff begin another long day. Management of the Anchorage area was realigned two years ago when the Greater Anchorage Area Borough and City of Anchorage merged to form the new Municipality of Anchorage. Sullivan has been mayor through it all. (Lael Morgan, Staff)

Left — Cindy Roberts, right, is a former model who started her own business and is now one of Alaska's only full-time fashion photographers. Business is brisk in ever-more-cosmopolitan Anchorage. (Lael Morgan, Staff)

Matanuska~Susitna Valleys

While other regions included in the Cook Inlet basin are strongly oriented toward the sea, the Matanuska and Susitna valleys — known for farming, mining and (lately) real estate — are focused almost totally on the land.

Fenced neatly by the Chugach Mountains, Talkeetna Mountains and Alaska Range, these rich lowlands, scoured time and again by advancing and retreating glaciers, host Alaska's most developed farmlands and not just a few of the state's land developers. Urged on by the possibility of a new state capital city near Willow, and by a lack of available real estate in the Anchorage bowl, entrepreneurs have begun to nibble on old homesteads and farmlands. The valleys are large, certainly, but rising property values (and escalating taxes) are beginning to alter the economics of agricultural use. Every time a farmer sells, it becomes a little harder for the others to resist.

Left — A typical Matanuska Valley farm, with Pioneer Peak, elevation 6,398 feet, in the background. (Garry Morris)

Right — Short-season hybrid corn planted at the University of Alaska's Experimental Farm, near Palmer. These plants are only 3 to 4 feet tall, but have produced mature ears. (Nancy Simmerman)

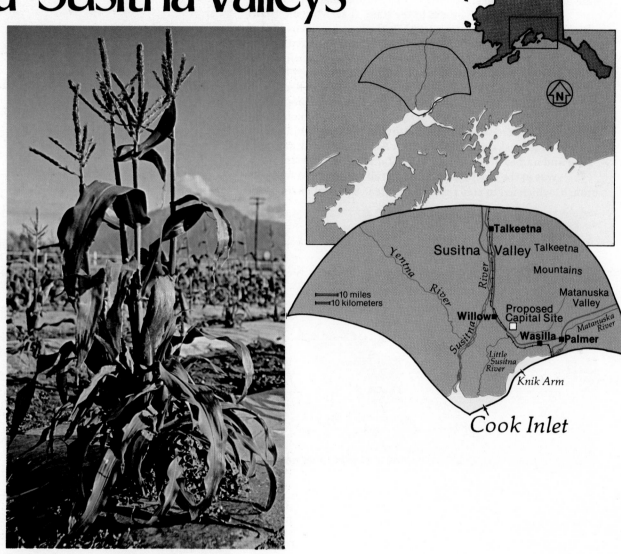

Talkeetna

Susitna Valley   Talkeetna
Mountains

Yentna River   Susitna River   Matanuska Valley

10 miles
10 kilometers

Proposed Capital Site

Willow

Matanuska River

Wasilla   Palmer

Little Susitna River

Knik Arm

Cook Inlet

Below — Many retired Alaskans live in Palmer at a modern state-supported Pioneers' Home — one of three major retirement homes in the state. (Lael Morgan, Staff)

Right — Palmer, population 1,643, is the commercial capital of the Matanuska and Susitna valleys, at least until a new state capital is built nearby. Palmer is 37 miles northwest of Anchorage on the Glenn Highway; an agricultural-supply town thought to have been named for George Palmer, a Knik Arm trader who worked the area in the late 1800's. (Nancy Simmerman)

Lower right — A few miles southwest of Palmer is the ghost town of Matanuska, established as an Alaska Railroad station in 1914 and named after the nearby Matanuska River. Matanuska was at the junction of the main rail line and a Matanuska branch, which led to coal fields in the area. (Marty Loken, Staff)

Left — Aerial view of the Matanuska Valley, with Knik Glacier and Knik River in the background. The glacier begins on Mount Marcus Baker in the Chugach Mountains and trends 30 miles west to a terminus 20 miles southeast of Palmer. (Nancy Simmerman)

Below — The valleys are hardly known for their timber industry, but this sawmill near Palmer is busy cutting the area's tall cottonwoods — an underrated species, according to the mill operator — for building construction. (Marty Loken, Staff)

The Talkeetna Mountains, once the site of considerable mining activity, today offer myriad recreational opportunities for Cook Inletters.

Left — In the winter and spring Hatcher Pass is a good spot to test snow machines and sled dogs. This team belongs to Joe Redington Sr., "Father of the Iditarod Race," who lives in Knik. Hatcher Pass, elevation 3,886 feet, is traversed by a 55-mile road that loops 20 miles northwest from the Glenn Highway near Palmer, winds over the pass, then meanders 35 miles west to the George Parks Highway near Willow. The Hatcher Pass road is suitable for auto travel only between June 15 and September 15. (Neil and Betty Johannsen)

Above — One of the region's favorite hang-gliding areas is Hatcher Pass, where flyers are treated to ideal takeoff spots, treeless landings and great scenery. (Theodore Bell)

Right — Independence Mine, near Hatcher Pass, is one of several inactive gold mines in the Talkeetna Mountains. Other mines along the Hatcher Pass road — an early mining trail — include Grubstake, Lucky Shot, War Baby and Gold Chord. Mining activity ended with the beginning of the Second World War. (Garry Morris)

The Talkeetna Mountains range from 6,000 to 8,800 feet, extending north-south 100 miles and east-west about 80 miles — bounded on the north by Broad Pass and the Nenana River; on the east by the Susitna River and Tyone Creek; on the south by Matanuska River; and on the west by the Chulitna and Susitna rivers.

Left — Three backpackers explore high country in the Talkeetnas. (Neal Menschel)

Right — Matanuska Glacier, a 27-mile-long ice field flowing from the Chugach Mountains, marks the headwaters of the Matanuska River 46 miles northeast of Palmer. The glacier is one of the most accessible in Southcentral Alaska, with its snout close to the Glenn Highway. (Pete Martin)

Lowland areas in the Matanuska and Susitna valleys — especially Susitna Flats and Eklutna Flats — are favorite areas for waterfowl hunting (whether with camera or shotgun).
Below — Watching for geese in Matanuska Valley. (Nancy Simmerman)
Right — Canada geese and snow geese in flight over Matanuska Valley. (Tom Walker)
Far right — A hunter and his Labrador retriever cross Eklutna Flats, near the head of Knik Arm, 25 miles northeast of Anchorage. (June Mackie, reprinted from *ALASKA*® magazine)

Far left — The Susitna River, "Big Su," is a 260-mile-long waterway that dominates the Susitna Valley and tests the course-choosing abilities of riverboaters. The meandering river begins high in the Alaska Range. (Sepp Weber, reprinted from *ALASKA*® magazine)

Left — Aerial view of the Susitna Valley, including the George Parks Highway, Wasilla (center), Lucile Lake (left) and Wasilla Lake (right). Wasilla, with an area population of about 1,600, is a roadside community 11 miles west of Palmer. The area between Palmer and Willow is growing and changing rapidly, partly because of real-estate speculation related to the proposed new state capital city, to be built at a site near the upper right corner of this photograph. (Nancy Simmerman)

Far left — Detail of an old barn in the Matanuska Valley.
(Neil and Betty Johannsen)

Left — Knik, once a bustling trading post on the north shore
of Knik Arm, has been reduced to just a few of the original
buildings, including the Knik Museum and Sled Dog Mushers'
Hall of Fame — formerly the town pool hall.
(Marty Loken, Staff)

Above, upper left, top — Signs of the times in the Matanuska
and Susitna valleys. (Marty Loken, Staff)

Above — The Alaska Railroad, whose construction created several towns in the Matanuska-Susitna valley area, presents several excellent views of Mount McKinley as it winds north through the valleys, climbing gradually to Broad Pass in the Alaska Range, then descending into the Interior. (Neil and Betty Johannsen)

Right — A fish wheel along the Susitna River. (Third Eye Photography)

Far Right — Talkeetna, population about 300, is the northernmost town in Cook Inlet country — and some townspeople would probably argue that they have nothing to do with Cook Inlet. The town is on The Alaska Railroad, near the spot where the Talkeetna and Chulitna rivers flow into the Susitna River. A pioneer mining and trapping community, Talkeetna has managed to retain much of its early-day pioneer atmosphere. (Marty Loken, Staff)

The West Side

This is the "other side" of Cook Inlet, well-known to relatively few Cook Inletters. The West Side, as we call it, stretches south along the inlet from Susitna Flats to Kamishak Bay, bordered on the east by crests of the Alaska Range and Aleutian Range. This is Cook Inlet's wild side — fewer people and more restless volcanoes than any other corner of the region.
Left — Although generally considered a mountainous area, the West Side has its flat spots, such as this meandering river drainage near Tyonek, southwest of Anchorage. (John and Margaret Ibbotson)
Right — Tyonek is the largest (and just about the only) community on the west side of Cook Inlet, with about 200 residents. Villagers several years ago leased some land on their reservation to oil companies for a test-drilling program. Results were apparently negative, but the villagers made more than a few dollars — investing much of it in new village facilities. Tyonek is in the geographic middle of mineral activities . . . present and future. Cook Inlet's offshore drilling rigs are almost due south of the village, and to the north are the much-discussed Beluga coal fields, controlled by the Cook Inlet Native Association and under consideration for eventual development. In the background of this photograph is Mount Susitna, 4,396 feet, in the Alaska Range. (Nancy Simmerman)

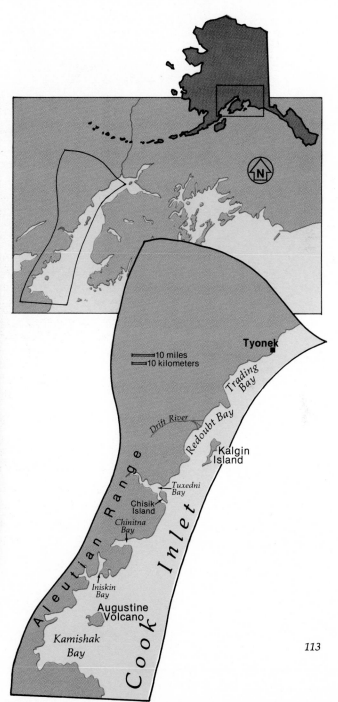

113

Above and above right — The west side of Cook Inlet is an ideal spot for fishermen, hunters and hikers — many of whom fly to the area from Anchorage. Alexander Lake Lodge, 46 miles north of Tyonek, is one such retreat. (Neil and Betty Johannsen) *Right* — A semipermanent Alaskan hunting camp, complete with wood stove. (Leland Brun)

Left — Hugh Fleischer displays a Cook Inlet pink salmon. The lower inlet — both sides — is a good area for both sport and commercial fishermen. (Neil and Betty Johannsen)
Above — Fall colors in a small stream on the west side of Cook Inlet. (Gary Gunkel)

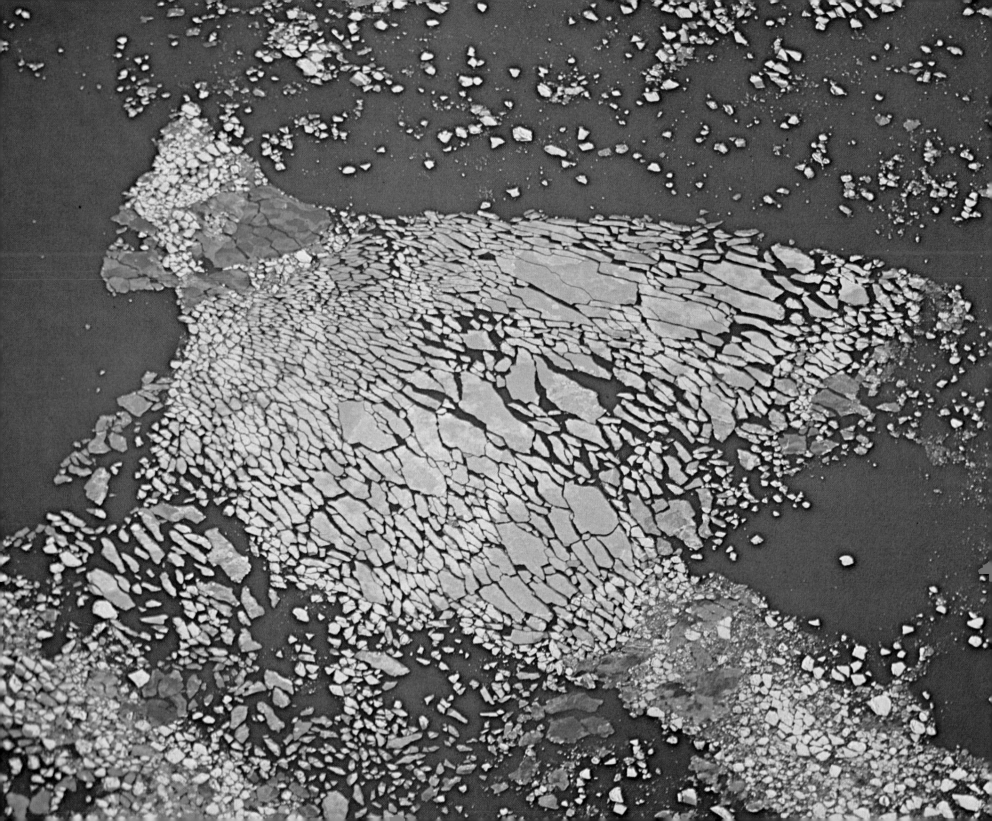

Left — Ice floes that clog Cook Inlet are seldom considered beautiful, but now and then the ice forms an interesting pattern. See the bird? (John and Margaret Ibbotson)

Above — An ARCO tanker calls at the Drift River loading facility, southwest of Tyonek in Redoubt Bay. Photograph was taken in February. (John and Margaret Ibbotson)

Kalgin Island, 22 miles west of Kenai, is one of four major islands in Cook Inlet.
Below — Skookum curls up in an old tire during the fishing-tender trip from Kenai Peninsula to Kalgin. (Marydith Beeman)
Right — Susan Beeman does her correspondence school homework on remote Kalgin Island. (Marydith Beeman)
Lower right — Red Beeman, a Cook Inlet set-netter, with a collection of fishing floats on Kalgin Island. (Marydith Beeman)

118

Chisik Island, southwest of Kalgin Island
at the mouth of Tuxedni Bay, 55 miles
southwest of Kenai, is a summer bird
rookery, and seasonal home for some
commercial salmon fishermen.
Left — Black-legged kittiwakes and
cormorants. The kittiwakes, oceanic
gulls, build their nests of grass and sod
on ledges, usually in colonies.
Cormorants are large, blackish, slender-
billed water birds, which often perch with
their necks in an "S."
(Nancy Simmerman)
Above — The Snug Harbor cannery, on
the west coast of Chisik Island, where
some Cook Inlet drift boats call.
(Lael Morgan, Staff)

Several major air passes, including Lake Clark Pass, Merrill Pass and Rainy Pass, cut through the Aleutian and Alaska ranges on the west side of Cook Inlet.

Left — Lake Clark Pass, 1,000 feet, is 50 miles west-northwest of Kenai and provides access to its namesake from Cook Inlet. (Bureau of Land Management)

Lower left — Shamrock Glacier, near Merrill Pass in the Chigmit Mountains. The glacier trends north 13 miles to its terminus between Chakachamna and Kenebuna lakes, 55 miles west of Tyonek. (Lael Morgan, Staff)

Below — The Tusks, near 3,180-foot Merrill Pass in the Alaska Range. The pass was named for R. H. Merrill, a pioneer aviator who discovered the route. (John and Margaret Ibbotson)

Right — Ptarmigan Valley, approaching 3,400-foot Rainy Pass in the Alaska Range. (Tom Walker)

120

Above — Directly west of Homer and north of Augustine Volcano is Iniskin Bay, a 10-mile-long estuary that was supposedly named for Enochkin, a Russian trader who had a post in the area. This view is to the northwest, toward the inner bay. (Garvan Bucaria)
Right — Ridges near the south entrance of Iniskin Bay, with Augustine Volcano in the background. (Lael Morgan, Staff)
Far right — A grizzly sow and cubs near the head of Kamishak Bay, 88 miles southwest of Homer — almost directly west of the south tip of Kenai Peninsula. (Tom Walker)

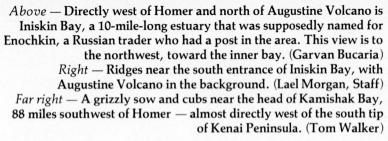

Saving the most dramatic until last in this section . . . the West Side's several volcanoes.

Left — Augustine Volcano, rising from Cook Inlet 70 miles southwest of Homer, during its January 25-February 6, 1976, eruption. Augustine has been one of the region's lively volcanoes, with eruptions in 1812, 1883, 1902, 1935, 1964 and 1976. The two most recent eruptions spread ash over much of the Cook Inlet basin. (Gary Gunkel)

Above — Another view of Augustine Volcano. (Gary Gunkel)

Right — Redoubt Volcano, 10,197 feet, 52 miles west of Kenai, was active in 1778, 1966, 1967 and 1968 . . . and probably several other years between 1778 and 1966. (Lael Morgan, Staff)

Lower right — Iliamna Volcano, south of Redoubt Volcano and about the same height (10,016 feet), was active in 1778 and 1779, and erupted in 1867. (Tom Walker)

Far right — A huge and ominous mushroom cloud swept over Cook Inlet during the 1976 eruption of Augustine. (Gary Gunkel)

Wilderness Resources

Mammals, birds, fish, minerals, trees and shrubs of the Cook Inlet region

Left — **A mature cow moose on the Kenai Peninsula, where the largest members of the deer family are abundant.**
(Tom Walker)
Above — **A big bull moose. Best spot in the Cook Inlet region for the animals is probably the Kenai National Moose Range, an ideal 1.7-million-acre habitat. (John and Margaret Ibbotson)**

The Cook Inlet region increasingly may be thought of as a place for people, but it's also a rich environment for most of Alaska's other mammals — large and small. Here are some of the larger mammals to be found in the area:

MOOSE (*Alces alces*) — This, the largest deer, is one of the most prominent and most important large mammals of the Cook Inlet basin. The Alaska subspecies is the largest of the genus, and the Kenai Peninsula moose was earlier believed to be the largest of Alaska's moose. (The peninsula's moose are large, but not necessarily *largest*.)

Moose adapt well to man's presence and virtually all towns and villages of the Cook Inlet basin have moose in and about them almost year-round. In winter especially, moose are visible in the outskirts of many towns: they find the snow-cleared roads and walks convenient, and as a change from willow and birch, their most important natural foods, browse upon remnants of vegetable gardens and on other cultivated plants.

Despite the moose's ability to live near man, habitat is critical if large numbers of this animal are to be preserved. In 1941 President Franklin D. Roosevelt set aside 1.7 million acres of the Kenai Peninsula to become the Kenai National Moose Range, where tree crushers, log sales and controlled burns set back tree succession to provide the plants upon which moose browse.

Top — **A bull caribou. The Cook Inlet region is not an important area of Alaska for these animals. (John and Margaret Ibbotson)**
Above — **Two caribou in the region. (Tom Walker)**

CARIBOU (*Rangifer tarandus*) — The Cook Inlet basin historically has not been, nor is it today, an important area for caribou. Caribou from the Talkeetna Mountains and from the Nelchina River area occasionally wander through the upper Susitna River Valley, as do caribou from the Broad Pass region in the Alaska Range. The entire west side of Cook Inlet, from about the Yentna River south to Cape Douglas, from the summit of the Chigmit Mountains to salt water, is virtually barren of caribou.

U.S. Biological Survey assistant Wilfred H. Osgood visited Cook Inlet in 1900, searching for information on wildlife. He found a small herd of Barren Ground caribou on the Kenai Peninsula, but they had become extinct by about 1913. Uncontrolled hunting and fire probably were the cause.

In May 1965, 15 caribou were captured in the Nelchina basin and released near the Chickaloon River. In April 1966, 29 more were caught in the Nelchina and released at Watson Lake, near Sterling. Both transplants were successful, and the Kenai Peninsula herd now numbers approximately 300 animals. They are found mostly within the Kenai National Moose Range.

Dall sheep are found in several areas within the Cook Inlet basin. (Tom Walker)

DALL SHEEP (*Ovis dalli*) — These pure-white sheep are found in the Kenai, Chugach and Talkeetna Mountains that rim the Cook Inlet basin. Visitors can see them from the Sterling Highway, in the Cooper Landing Closed Area adjacent to Kenai Lake, as well as at Sheep Mountain, which borders the Glenn Highway at the headwaters of the Matanuska River.

Dall sheep live almost entirely in the alpine zone, although they may range locally into brush and timber. They need cliffs and rugged rock outcrops as sanctuaries from predators. Most important habitat need seems to be an acceptable winter climate, which means cold temperatures, wind and moderate snowfall. Cold keeps the snow light and powdery, while winds remove it from ridges where the animals feed on exposed forage — bunch grass, other grasses, sedges, forbs, willow and dryas.

Left — **Mountain goats, mainly a coastal species, are scattered in high areas of the region. (Tom Walker)**
Lower left — **Wolves have appeared most everywhere in the Cook Inlet area. (Tom Walker)**

MOUNTAIN GOAT (*Oreamnos americanus*) — Spike-horned and white-coated, mountain goats are found in the Kenai, Chugach and Talkeetna Mountains. A few stragglers are found almost to McKinley Park. But the goat is mostly a coastal species in Alaska, where it seems to do best along a narrow strip from the Kenai Peninsula south and east.

Mountain goats, which are not true goats but allies of the true antelopes, live in the high mountains, where they walk on narrow ledges, projecting pinnacles and talus slopes. Mountain goats have no apparent fear of heights. In some areas goat and Dall sheep habitat overlap, with the goats preferring and remaining in the more rugged areas.

WOLF (*Canis lupus*) — Wolves are found through the Cook Inlet basin, even near the outskirts of Anchorage and other large cities. They disappeared from the Kenai Peninsula about 1915, probably due to a rabies epidemic. They reappeared there in the early 1960's, and were given complete protection until the early 1970's, when their numbers reached an estimated 100 or more. Limited hunting and seasonal trapping was restored.

Today there may be 125 to 150 wolves living on the Kenai Peninsula. Good numbers are also found in the Chugach and Talkeetna Mountains, throughout the Susitna River Valley, and along the west side of Cook Inlet.

BLACK BEAR (*Ursus americanus*) — Black bears are common throughout the Cook Inlet basin except for the extreme southwest, south of the tree line, where the coastal brown bear is found. The distribution of our most common bear coincides with the distribution of forests, but not any forest will do. Blackies prefer open forests, where there are fruit-bearing shrubs and herbs, lush grasses and succulent herbs. Extensive open areas, like those of the Kamishak region of the southwestern Cook Inlet basin, are generally avoided by these omniverous black foragers. One of the areas of greatest abundance of black bears in Alaska has long been the Kenai Peninsula. But even here black bear numbers vary considerably from time to time.

BROWN/GRIZZLY BEAR (*Ursus arctos*) — The brown/grizzly bears of Alaska are the world's largest terrestrial carnivores. They're called brown bears when along the coast, and grizzly bears in the Interior regions. Scientists say they're one and the same highly variable species of bear. Hump-shouldered, bow-legged, dish-faced, and with long claws, they are easily distinguished from their smaller cousin, the black bear. Color may vary from light yellow to nearly black.

Brown bears are probably as abundant in areas of the Cook Inlet basin unaltered by man as they were during presettlement days. They have been increasing slightly on the Kenai Peninsula, and the number of big bears in the Susitna River Valley is high.

Brown/grizzly bears are probably the least compatible with humans of any of Alaska's wildlife, and without special consideration their numbers are markedly reduced wherever important human occupation and confrontation occur.

Slow he might be, but the porcupine (sometimes called a quill pig) is far from defenseless. (George Moerlein, reprinted from ALASKA®magazine)

SMALL MAMMALS

Cook Inlet has a wide variety of small mammals, ranging from the tiny shrew, through the various fur bearers, porcupine and snowshoe hare.

SNOWSHOE OR VARYING HARE (*Lepus americanus*) — This is a keystone species for many others. The lynx cycle follows that of the hare, and foxes, wolverines, owls, raptors all utilize the snowshoe hare for food.

Snowshoe hares are found in wooded parts of Alaska from Prince William Sound and Cook Inlet north to, and slightly beyond, the limit of spruce. These animals are common throughout the brushy and wooded areas of the Cook Inlet basin, and, as elsewhere, their numbers rise and fall in cycles that approximate 10 years.

PORCUPINE (*Erethizon dorsatum*) — Common throughout the Cook Inlet basin, the porcupine is found in all timbered parts of Alaska except for some islands.

Unaggressive, harmless if left alone, the porcupine goes through life largely ignoring other animals. If a young and dumb, or an especially hungry predator attacks, the porcupine bows its head stubbornly, turns its slashing quill-equipped tail toward the enemy, and makes it almost impossible for the predator to avoid catching a face full of quills.

RED FOX (*Vulpes vulpes*) — The red fox, cross fox, silver fox and black fox are all the same species — and all may be found in a single litter, with the black fox being the rarest of the four.

Found throughout the Cook Inlet basin, red foxes are one of the most common of the predators. Wintertime reveals their trails, wandering for miles in the snow as they search for mice, snowshoe hares, birds. They dig their dens on well-drained hillsides, usually with several entrances. From three to six pups are born in May.

WOLVERINE (*Gulo gulo*) — This largest of the land-dwelling members of the weasel family is found from sea level to the mountaintops throughout the Cook Inlet basin. It isn't abundant, but it isn't rare, either. It is usually regarded as a wilderness species, but it seems to be able to live near metropolitan areas — as it does in the Chugach State Park, near Anchorage.

MARTEN (*Martes americana*) — This is the American equivalent of the European sable, with the softest and loveliest of furs. From deep brown to a light orange, with a whitish to orange throat patch, this member of the weasel family weighs two to three pounds and measures about 25 inches, of which one-third is its bushy tail.

Marten are most common in thick spruce forests, wherever they grow in the Cook Inlet basin.

LAND OTTER (*Lutra canadensis*) — This large weasel family member also is adapted to aquatic life and is found in all major watercourses of the Cook Inlet basin. Long-bodied, measuring from 40 to 45 inches and weighing 18 to 20 pounds, the land otter is a powerful animal. Its short legs give it a humped inchwormlike appearance as it travels on land, but it is the epitome of grace in the water.

MINK (*Mustela vison*) — Usually weighing less than two pounds, this small member of the weasel family inhabits all watersheds of Cook Inlet. Long-bodied and short-legged, like others of its clan, the mink has the ability to live in water or on land, eating fish, mice, birds and rabbits.

WEASEL (*Mustela* sp.) — Both the least weasel and ermine are found throughout the Cook Inlet basin. Both turn white in winter and ermine is the common name for them in that stage. Tiny, slender-bodied predators, they feed on mice, birds, squirrels, even rabbits.

Lower left — **Red foxes are found throughout the Cook Inlet region.** (Helen Rhode) *Below* — **The snowshoe hare seems to be food for everyone — the lynx, fox, wolverine, owl and others.** (Tom Walker)

BEAVER (*Castor canadensis*) — A heavy-bodied, aquatic rodent found throughout the Cook Inlet basin. It lives in lakes, rivers or ponds, where it can find sufficient food.

MUSKRAT (*Ondatra zibethica*) — Nearly two feet long, this water-dwelling rodent is found in all drainages of the Cook Inlet basin, and is occasionally mistaken for a beaver. However, when swimming the sculling tail of the muskrat is usually a giveaway.

COYOTE (*Canis latrans*) — Indications are that coyotes moved into Alaska shortly after the turn of the century. They increased, became entrenched and reached a peak in 1940, when an estimated 20,000 were scattered across the state.

Since 1940 their numbers have decreased, but they persist in good numbers on the Kenai Peninsula, east into the Copper River Valley and in both Matanuska and Susitna River valleys.

Beavers are found most everywhere, in lakes, ponds and rivers. (George Herben)

LYNX (*Lynx lynx*) — These short-bodied, long-legged wild cats in recent years developed a great value in Alaska, with their fur bringing premium prices — $200 to $300 a pelt. (Trapping is now restricted.)

Lynx depend heavily upon snowshoe hares, and where hares increase, lynx are almost sure to increase, too. They also feed on all species of birds, mice, and, on occasion, salmon or carrion.

These handsome cats are found throughout the Cook Inlet basin, even though they are seldom seen because they are largely nocturnal. Easiest way to know of the presence of lynx is to see their tracks in new snow.

MISCELLANEOUS LAND MAMMALS — The Cook Inlet basin also is home to a number of small and large rodents and insectivores, including: red squirrel (*Tamiasciurus hudsonicus*); flying squirrel (*Glaucomys sabrinus*); ground squirrel (*Citellus undulatus*); hoary marmot (*Marmota caligata*); collared pika (*Ochotona collaris*); red-backed vole or mouse (*Clethrionomys* sp.); shrew (*Sorex* sp.); and little brown myotis (*Myotis lucifugus*).

Above — **The lynx population follows the ups and downs of the snowshoe hare, its favorite food source. (John Crawford)** *Right* — **Another creature found in the region — the hoary marmot. (John and Margaret Ibbotson)**

134

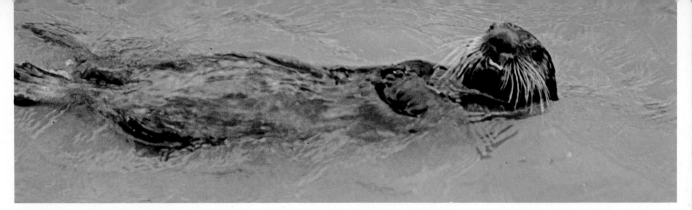

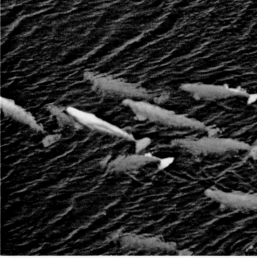

SEA MAMMALS

HARBOR OR SPOTTED SEAL (*Phoca vitulina*) — Harbor seals are found throughout Cook Inlet and its bays and fjords: they even ascend the larger rivers for some miles, and may appear in lakes near salt water.

These common seals haul out on offshore rocks and sand bars that are exposed during low tide. They use flat beach areas, large rock outcrops worn smooth by surf, and floating ice that breaks off glaciers. Occasionally 100 or more seals may be seen hauled out in one place.

The mud flats of the Susitna River at the head of Cook Inlet are traditional pupping grounds, and several thousand seals annually appear here in late May and early June. Other pupping grounds are found in the Kustatan area, just below West Foreland, on and below Kalgin Island, in Chinitna Bay — especially on the mud flats at the head of the bay and at the head of Kachemak Bay.

SEA OTTER (*Enhydra lutris*) — Explorer Vitus Bering's crews returned to Russia with sea otter furs and soon after the lure of these fine furs brought death and destruction to all but a handful of Alaska's sea otters.

Since 1911, when sea otters were finally protected (by an almost inadvertency in the International Fur Seal Treaty), these interesting animals have increased to near original numbers throughout Alaska, with man's help in bridging the wide gaps where natural spread failed.

Cook Inlet is the northernmost part of the animal's range. The inlet above Ninilchik never has supported sea otters because they need clear water: the silt clear-water line for the inlet is roughly at Ninilchik, depending upon the size of the tide.

STELLER SEA LION (*Eumetopias jubata*) — Sea lions are not abundant in Cook Inlet, although stragglers spill over from the large population of these big seal-like animals that live along the outer coast of the Kenai Peninsula and in the Barren Islands.

PORPOISE (*Phocoena phocoena*) — Harbor porpoises are seen frequently in Cook Inlet, especially in the Kachemak Bay area.

BELUGA (*Delphinapterus leucas*) — Each spring many of these small white whales arrive in Cook Inlet for the summer; they probably exist mostly on salmon. In late fall they move out and are seen no more until the following spring.

Aerial surveys made to count belugas in the inlet have resulted in estimates of 300 to 500, but the numbers may be considerably higher.

LARGE WHALES — Cook Inlet waters do not attract many large whales. Most common species is probably the minke or little piked whale, smallest of the baleen whales, with a maximum length of about 33 feet. Occasionally seen south of Kalgin Island, and fairly common in Kachemak Bay, some individuals may remain in an area feeding for days or even weeks.

Top left — **The sea otter, nearly wiped out by Russian fur traders, has made a strong comeback since being protected in 1911.** (Dr. Nicholas Deely)
Top — **Steller sea lions are seen infrequently in Cook Inlet.** (T. C. Newby)
Above — **Beluga whales inhabit the inlet each summer, feeding primarily on salmon.** (Leslie Nakashima)

135

BIRDS OF THE COOK INLET BASIN

Little information is available on Cook Inlet's birds because few studies have been made and ornithological records mainly reflect lists published by various observers. However, the wide diversity of environments in the basin furnish habitats for a large variety of birds. Sea birds are perhaps the most abundant on a year-round basis, with waterfowl (ducks, geese, swans) also abundant seasonally.

The spruce-birch forest habitat that ranges to near timber-line level, about 2,000 feet, of the Kenai, Alaska, Chugach and Talkeetna Mountains is a year-round home for relatively few species of birds, such as the raven, chickadee, redpoll, Canada and Steller's jay, magpie and several woodpeckers; but this habitat is home for many others in summer.

At least 105 species of birds have been observed at various locations around and in the salt-water habitat of Cook Inlet, including island nesting rookeries, feeding areas in salt water, salt marshes and beaches.

A number of marshes important to birds surround the inlet. At Palmer Hay Flats, geese, swans and ducks stop to feed and rest during spring and fall migration, and some remain to nest. Other migration stops for ducks and geese are Goose Bay, Susitna Flats, Trading Bay, Redoubt Bay, and Chickaloon Flats. (As many as 20,000 or more Canada geese and 500 swans congregate at Chickaloon Flats, which also is used extensively by sandhill cranes during migration.) Potter, Eagle River and Portage marshes are stopovers for ducks, geese and swans, as are the Fox River Flats at the head of Kachemak Bay.

Other waterfowl concentration points include Kalgin Island, the tidal flats near the mouth of the Kenai River, Kustatan marsh and the Silver Salmon Creek area. Kachemak Bay, Halibut Cove, China Poot Bay, Sadie Cove, Tutka Bay, Seldovia Bay and Aurora Lagoon are used by waterfowl spring, summer, fall, and by some birds throughout the winter.

Above — **Snow geese stop to feed and rest near the mouth of Kenai River.** (Roy A. Mullin)
Right — **Sandhill cranes in flight near Anchorage.** (Robert Maurer)

136

Far left —
Common murres in Kachemak Bay. (Jim Rearden, Staff)
Left — **Bonaparte gulls nesting at Potter Marsh, south of Anchorage. (Nancy Simmerman)**

Auks, murres and puffins form a large part of the water bird population of Cook Inlet. Minor nesting colonies in the Cook Inlet basin are found at Gull Island, in Kachemak Bay, at Elizabeth and Perl Islands at the tip of the Kenai Peninsula, and on Gull Island at Chinitna Bay.

Largest sea bird colony of the inlet is at Chisik Island, in Tuxedni Bay, on the west side of the inlet. The island is a federal wildlife refuge for the swarms of sea birds found there in summer. The black-legged kittiwake, a small gull, is one of the most abundant nesters.

Duck Island, which lies on the east side of Chisik Island, is also a summer nesting area.

Upland birds of the Cook Inlet basin include willow and rock ptarmigan, spruce grouse, and myriad small birds — swallows, jays, magpies, crows, titmice, nuthatches, creepers, dippers, wrens, thrushes, warblers, shrikes, vireos, wood warblers, grosbeaks, finches, sparrows and buntings.

Tufted puffins in the Kachemak Bay region of Kenai Peninsula. (Jim Rearden, Staff)

A common upland bird of the region is the willow ptarmigan. (Tom Walker)

UNDER THE INLET, AND ON THE SEASHORES . . .

The Cook Inlet region is rich in marine life — especially the lower half of the inlet. Kachemak Bay, in particular, is one of the better marine environments to be found in terms of its abundance of life. Here are a few examples from the Cook Inlet region. . . .

Far left, top — King crabs may be huge by the time they reach your plate, but they start out as thumbnail-sized critters. These two were photographed at Kachemak Bay. (Nancy Simmerman)

Far left, bottom — Three major species found in Cook Inlet are, from left, king, tanner and Dungeness crab. (Nancy Simmerman)

Left — Five species of salmon. From top to bottom they are king (chinook); red (sockeye); chum (dog); silver (coho); and pink (humpback). These were taken in July from Cook Inlet. (Nancy Simmerman)

Lower left — A halibut from the Kalgin Island area. (Marydith Beeman)

Below — Razor clams are Cook Inlet's most sought-after clam. (Jim Rearden, Staff)

Bottom — Salmon spawning near Moose Pass, on the Kenai Peninsula. (Louise Doxtator)

138

Left — Three species of shrimp found in Cook Inlet. Top to bottom are spot, pink and coonstripe shrimp.
(Dennis Bromley)
Below — An octopus from the waters of Kachemak Bay.
(Nancy Simmerman)

MINERAL RESOURCES

Today the Cook Inlet region is not an important mining area. The early years, however, were different, with much mining activity. This was about the first place where gold and oil were exploited in Alaska, and reserves of coal, chrome and iron are extensive.

The Cook Inlet-Susitna River region includes five mining districts — Anchorage, Redoubt, Valdez Creek, Willow Creek and Yentna.

The region is entirely within the Pacific Mountain system. Its west and north borders are along the east and south slopes of the Alaska Range and its southeastern boundary is the crest of the lower, but no less rugged, Chugach Mountains. The region includes another highland area, the Talkeetna Mountains, a nearly circular mountain mass with most peaks between 6,000 and 8,300 feet in elevation. The eastern boundary of the region is an ill-defined divide in the western part of the poorly drained lake-speckled Copper River Lowland. A somewhat poorly drained area, the Cook Inlet-Susitna Lowland is an extension of Cook Inlet; it separates the southern Alaska Range from the Talkeetna Mountains. Low mountains and ranges of hills rise from a few hundred to a few thousand feet above the lowland, particularly near the foothills of the Alaska Range.

Ice completely covered this part of Alaska during the Pleistocene, spreading from the Alaska Range far out to sea. (Ice still covers the highest parts of the mountains, and valley glaciers, one more than 35 miles long, extend far from their source areas.)

Gold and silver have been recovered from lodes in many parts of the region and a little copper from deposits in the Redoubt and Valdez Creek districts. These and other lodes have also been investigated as possible sources of antimony, iron, chromite, molybdenum, copper, lead, and zinc. Float samples collected in the southwestern part of the Yentna district contained as much as 60 parts per million (about 1.7 ounces per ton) of gold associated with chalcopyrite, arsenopyrite and other sulfides. The only large-scale production, however, was from the Willow Creek area north of Palmer, where between 1909 and World War II gold-bearing quartz veins in the southern border zone of the Talkeetna batholith were the source of about 404,425 ounces of gold, 5% of Alaska's total lode gold output. Minor amounts of gold, silver, and base metals have been produced from the upper Chulitna area near the Alaska Railroad. Total metallic resources are large and, in the future, might well become important to the Alaskan economy.

Placer gold was discovered in the region in the late 19th century, and mining has been carried on continuously since the early 1900's. Output was probably about 250,000 ounces, or less than 70% of the lode-gold production. The bulk of the placer gold has come from streams that drain the Dutch Hills and Fairview Mountain in the Yentna district, from Valdez Creek in the Valdez Creek district, and from Crow Creek in the Anchorage district.

Other mineral resources that have been exploited include pumice from Augustine Volcano, minor amounts of ceramic clay and agricultural lime from near Anchorage, a little gypsum and clay from Sheep Mountain in the upper Matanuska Valley, soapstone (for carving) from near Palmer, and large amounts of construction materials along railroad and highway routes and near Anchorage. Limestone deposits in the northwestern part of the Valdez Creek district and in the Matanuska Valley east of Palmer have been investigated as possible sources of raw material for portland cement.

Oil and gas produced from fields in Cook Inlet and southeast of it in the Homer and Hope districts of the Kenai Peninsula region have far outshadowed all other mineral commodities in value; since 1959 the value of this production has been greater than $1¼ billion and, until start-up of the trans-Alaska oil constituted almost the entire oil and gas production of the state.

There are large resources (more than 2½ billion short tons) of bituminous and subbituminous coal in the Matanuska Valley of the Willow Creek district, in the Tyonek-Beluga River area of the Redoubt district, in the central part of the Yentna district, and near Broad Pass in the Valdez Creek district. Extensive mining has been carried on only in the Matanuska Valley. — Edward H. Cobb, from *Mineral Resources and Geology of Alaska*, U.S. Geological Survey. □

Above left — Cook Inlet's production of petroleum has led other areas of the state, in terms of the value of minerals produced, for more than a decade. The region has now been overshadowed by the North Slope, but additional fields will probably be drilled in the not-distant future, now that federal offshore tracts are about to be leased in Lower Cook Inlet. (John B. Noble)

Above — Independence Mine, one of several earlier gold mines in the Talkeetna Mountains. The Willow Creek area accounted for about 5% of Alaska's total lode gold output from 1909 to the Second World War, when most operations ceased. (Al Romaszewski)

Left — Erickson gold mine, an old operation near Girdwood, south of Anchorage. (Sharon Paul, Staff)

Above — Low-growing willows along the shores of Turnagain Arm, near Anchorage. (Third Eye Photography)

Right — A spruce forest near Kachemak Bay, on the Kenai Peninsula. White spruce is the Cook Inlet region's most important tree, in terms of commercial value. (Nancy Simmerman)

TREES AND SHRUBS

IN THE FORESTS . . .

Nearly all of the commercial production of wood products in Alaska is from 10 species of trees, eight of which are found in the Cook Inlet region . . . though not necessarily in commercial quantities. (Missing in the region are the stands of cedar and fir that contribute — along with other species — to the timber business in Southeastern Alaska.) Here's a list of major species in the Cook Inlet area:

·BLACK SPRUCE (*Picea mariana*) — Common from Kachemak Bay north around Cook Inlet and along the west side of the inlet to the Redoubt Volcano area. Usually small, 15 to 30 feet high, 3 to 6 inches in trunk diameter, with narrow pointed crown.

WHITE SPRUCE (*Picea glauca*) — Found from the Kenai area inland and north around the head of Cook Inlet and south to the Redoubt area. Most important tree of the spruce-birch Interior forest; 40 to 70 feet high and 6 to 18 inches in trunk diameter.

SITKA SPRUCE (*Picea sitchensis*) — Common along coastal areas from lower Cook Inlet from the Redoubt area south to Kamishak Bay. On the Kenai Peninsula this tree often hybridizes with white spruce to form Lutz spruce. Sitka spruce is one of the most valuable trees in Alaska (and the Cook Inlet region); up to 160 feet in height although heights rarely exceed 120 feet in the inlet region, and 3 to 5 feet in trunk diameter.

WESTERN HEMLOCK (*Tsuga heterophylla*) — Found in lower east Cook Inlet, south of Kachemak Bay, and around the south side and head of Turnagain Arm. A large evergreen becoming 100 to 150 feet tall and 2 to 4 feet in trunk diameter.

MOUNTAIN HEMLOCK (*Tsuga mertensiana*) — Common inland on the Kenai Peninsula, especially around the Kenai area, and around Turnagain Arm and the east side of Knik Arm. Also inland in the Tyonek area. Mountain hemlocks are 50 to 100 feet high and 10 to 30 inches in trunk diameter.

BALSAM POPLAR (*Populus balsamifera*) — Common in river valleys and flood plains on the Kenai Peninsula from Kachemak Bay north around Cook Inlet to the Redoubt area. A medium-sized deciduous tree, usually 30 to 50 feet high, with a straight trunk 4 to 12 inches in diameter.

BLACK COTTONWOOD (*Populus trichocarpa*) — Not easily distinguished from Balsam poplar . . . the two often hybridize where their ranges overlap. Found in coastal lowlands from the lower east side of the inlet north to the west side of the Susitna River. A large deciduous tree 80 to 100 feet tall, with a straight trunk about 3 feet in diameter.

QUAKING ASPEN (*Populus tremuloides*) — Common on well-drained slopes and in creek bottoms on the east side of the inlet from Kachemak Bay north around the head of the inlet, and south to the Redoubt area. A small to medium-sized deciduous tree commonly 20 to 40 feet tall, with a straight trunk 3 to 12 inches in diameter.

PAPER BIRCH (*Betula papyrifera*) — Found throughout the region from Kachemak Bay, slightly inland, north to Knik Arm and extending to the coast south to Redoubt area. Paper birch are small to medium-sized, usually 20 to 60 feet high and 4 to 12 inches in trunk diameter.

Not quite in the tree category are a variety of willows and alders that may — depending on growth — appear either as shrubs or trees. Among the shrub-trees are: Barclay willow (*Salix barclayi*); Bebb willow (*Salix bebbliana*); feltleaf willow (*Salix alaxensis*); grayleaf willow (*Salix glauca*); Scouler willow (*Salix scouleriana*); Sitka willow (*Salix sitchensis*); Sitka alder (*Alnus sinuata*); and thinleaf alder (*Alnus tenuifolia*).

Then, finally, we have a variety of shrubs that come from families which many people usually think of as trees. In the Cook Inlet region, they include: common juniper (*Juniperus communis*); diamond leaf willow (*Salix planifolia*); dwarf arctic birch (*Betula nana*); resin birch (*Betula glandulosa*); red-osier dogwood (*Cornus stolonifera*); Greene mountain-ash (*Sorbus scopulina*); and Sitka mountain-ash (*Sorbus sitchensis*). — M. Clark Fultz, U.S. Forest Service silvaculturist, compiled from the handbook, *Alaska Trees and Shrubs*. □

Aspens and blueberries. (Pete Martin)

Following page — **Augustine Volcano, photographed from Ursus Cove, Kamishak Bay. (David B. Andersen)**